SOME CATCH!

Thirty baseball gems capturing the humor and drama of the game

by

BILL SCHAEFER

May, 2023

Copyright@ 2023 by Bill Schaefer

All rights reserved

No part of this book may be reproduced without written permission of the author

Photo Credits: Cover photo of Willie Mays beautifully colorized by resident baseball artist, Don Stokes. View all of Don's artwork at the *Old-Time Baseball Colorizations* Facebook page.

Color restoration of Rube Waddell courtesy of artist Chris Whitehouse of *They Played in Color*. View all of Chris's artwork at: www.mancavepictures.com.

All other photos from Google search and/or public domain.

ISBN:

Printed in the United States of America
First paperback printing: July, 2023

DEDICATION

To my amazing wife, Susan, forever my inspiration and champion who believes in me totally, but never shy: "You can do better!"

To a couple of great new friends: Gary Livacari, creator of the best baseball website extant. His *Baseball History Comes Alive* gave me the opportunity to put some thoughts down on paper about the game I love—and a wonderful mentor! Also, the talented Michael Keedy, whose picture is next to the word, "eloquent" in the dictionary. Mikey never met a multifaceted sentence he didn't like. But once you read his essays, you'll say, "Man, this guy is some writer!"

And finally, four terrific friends of long standing: Dave Frankel, Joe Caroselli, Bob Tombs and Jim Montemurro. Respectively, three die hard (often disgruntled) Mets fans and the ultimate Dodgers fanatic. Never mind metrics, they know which players are getting it done!

CONTENTS

FOREWORD, by Michael Keedy vi
AUTHOR'S INTRODUCTION, by Bill Schaefer viii
EDITOR'S INTRODUCTION, by Gary Livacari x

"THIRTY "GEMS"

1. RUBE WADDELL: THE ULTIMATE ZANY 1
2. DON MATTINGLY: FAME SECOND TO FAITH AND FAMILY 6
3. BILL SCHAEFER'S TWENTY MINUTES WITH WILLIE MAYS 12
4. BASEBALL APPETIZERS FOR THE '21 SEASON 16
5. TRAGIC STORY OF BASEBALL'S UNFORTUNATE HALL-OF-FAMER, ERNIE LOMBARDI 21
6. BASEBALL'S CUTTING EDGE HUMOR: *"THE GLORY OF THEIR (FUNNY) LINES"* 25
7. THE STRANGE CASE OF VON McDANIEL 30
8. *BASEBALL, FUNNY SIDE UP!* 35
9. GIANTS, DODGERS AND A BRAWL FOR THE AGES 39
10. THE NEW YORK METS' FAMOUS "SIGN MAN" 43
11. TOM SEAVER INTERVIEW, PRELUDE TO A MIRACLE… AND MORE 48
12. THE AMAZING STORY OF REX BARNEY 53
13. RANDOM MUSINGS OF A LIFE-LONG GIANTS FAN 57
14. STAN MUSIAL: THE BEGINNING-THE CRISIS- THE THIRD MVP 62

15.	BASEBALL'S CONTRIBUTION TO THE LEXICON	67
16.	A MEMORABLE DAY AT YANKEE STADIUM	71
17.	THE TURBULENT LIFE OF HARRY "THE HAT" WALKER	75
18.	FLASHBACKS...AND WHO'S ON FIRST (on *your* all-time team)?	80
19.	SNAP SHOTS FROM A GIANTS FAN, THROUGH A SURREAL SEASON	85
20.	THE GREAT BASEBALL NAME GAME: "VINEGAR BEND" MIZELL	93
21.	ANOTHER EDITION OF BASEBALL'S FORGOTTEN STARS: "PISTOL" PETE REISER	98
22.	MEL OTT—*THE BIGGEST LITTLE GIANT*	103
23.	BOBO NEWSOM: A GREAT CHARACTER WITH A HEART TO MATCH	108
24.	SAILING THROUGH THE DECADES WITH THE YANKEE CLIPPER-PART ONE	111
25.	JOE DiMAGGIO, PART TWO DiMAG POST-WAR: *JOE, MARILYN, AND PAUL SIMON*	116
26.	THE CLOWN PRINCE OF BASEBALL: Al SCHACHT	122
27.	THE SHOT HEARD 'ROUND THE WORLD (THAT ALMOST WASN'T)	127
28.	AN UMPIRE'S UMPIRE	131
29.	EDDIE STANKY: *THE BRAT!*	136
30.	ONE MEMORABLE OPENING DAY AND STORY	141
	ABOUT THE AUTHOR	145

FOREWORD
by Michael Keedy

So many biographies, poems and encyclopedias have been written about our nation's most captivating pastime that the mosaic of baseball's storied history has begun to resemble a soggy finger-painting. An inquiring student of the game is often hard-pressed to select a work on this beloved sport that educates and entertains without sounding familiar, repetitive, and—well, routine.

This offering from Mr. Bill Schaefer is the rare and welcome exception. Indeed, what he calls "gems" are exactly that. The man does not exaggerate! He has managed to produce a treasury of fond and vivid memories from his transfixed, early days at the ballpark, from early childhood with his dearly departed dad. There isn't an ordinary vignette in the lot; nothing that might be confused with our eager student's previous encounters with baseball literature in any form.

In fact, the many profiles within cannot be duplicated by another writer, or summarily confirmed by references to "as told to" bios, stat books or other storehouses of mind-numbing trivia. Bill's book is one-of-a-kind, relying as it does upon his own observations and experiences in attending so many ball games as an impressionable kid, maturing adolescent, or contemplative adult over three-quarters of a century. Writing in an intimate, conversational style, he shares with the reader memorable quotations from literary giants and apt asides from baseball's greatest stars, more obscure participants (many of whom he interviewed), and hilarious diversions into baseball's lexicon, its madcap characters, and little-known but revealing and instructive episodes.

SOME CATCH!

As Bill Schaefer's fond friend and fellow writer, I am enchanted with the result. More importantly, I have no doubt you will savor this trove as I have. *Some Catch, Thirty Baseball Gems* promises to become an instant, constant companion to anyone who loves and appreciates the national pastime as much as our intrepid author so obviously does. Congratulations, Bill!

Michael H. Keedy
June, 2023

AUTHOR'S INTRODUCTION
by Bill Schaefer

My dad took me to my first game at the Polo Grounds on June 11, 1944 when I was six (wait, I can't be that old!). Actually, it was a double header and I asked him later if they ever played a triple header. I loved going to the Giants games through that season and the next, and through the first half of 1946, when the last vestiges of a big war had faded away. But I wasn't a fanatic just yet.

Then, on September 1, my father and I were in the upper deck behind home plate at the Polo Grounds for a Labor Day twin bill. In the opener, Bill Voiselle was throttling the (almost) pennant bound Brooklyn Dodgers 1-0 in the top of the eighth inning. Suddenly, I found myself riveted and hanging on every pitch. Then was shocked when Dixie Walker and Ed Stevens exploded back-to-back homers deep into the lower right field seats. Brooklyn won 3-1. And even though our beloved ball team was bringing up the rear in the senior circuit, my heart was broken.

Starting opening day, 1947, with full fanaticism raging, I kept score listening to Steve Ellis and Frankie Frisch doing the Giants games on WMCA. And was able to recount every at bat for both teams, just by looking at the players' names. I would scream at the radio and correct the announcers. That intensity lasted through high school, faded at Lehigh University when the teams left for California, and was rekindled when the Mets were born in 1962. But never at quite the fever pitch of those early days.

I'm still a long suffering Mets fan (great moments too), but now with a better perspective on the game. Writing about it has been a joy since fortuitously hooking up with *Baseball History Comes Alive* in 2020. I never dreamed an initial essay would lead to the book you are about to read.

SOME CATCH!

I've selected a diversified array of yarns, running the gamut of often hilarious baseball humor and including the pathos and drama inherent in the sport. The journey reaches back briefly to pre-1900 and touches a present day reference. But mostly you'll be reveling in the lively ball era through the early '70's; interrupting Tom Seaver running wind sprints in early 1969, at a dilapidated Connie Mack Stadium; and Willie Mays being ambushed by a local radio announcer, when he joined the Mets in 1973. The essays are also peppered with outrageous experiences at the ballpark with my dad that will be sure to trigger your own special memories. The bios include amazing players as well as legendary baseball characters: Rube Waddell was not only an extraordinary pitcher but also possessed a screwball personality like no other. Rube is in the lead-off spot.

Plenty of stats to be sure, but you won't be inundated. Just enough nuts and bolts to inform and entertain.

With judicious edits and wonderful photos provided by Gary Livacari, my fervent wish is that you will thoroughly enjoy this collection. The writing is geared to provide fast reads. So, if you do find a piece that doesn't particularly enthrall you--you'll be done in a hurry!

Thanks for turning the pages. Enjoy!

Bill Schaefer
Springfield, New Jersey
May 2023

EDITOR'S INTRODUCTION
by Gary Livacari

When I started the *Baseball History Comes Alive* website back in January 2016, my goal was to honor and preserve the glory days of baseball. I also sought to recapture the long-lost charm of the game. In recent years, I've found myself becoming increasingly disenchanted with the contemporary version. Was it the incessant rule changes? The influx of mega dollars? The loss of fundamentals? Laptops in the dugouts? (Ugh!). Being an "old-school guy," I never even warmed up to the designated hitter. As a National League fan, I begrudgingly came to tolerate it…that is, as long as it stayed put in the American League where it belonged. Alas, I've now been deprived of even that modest request.

As I embarked on this mission, I knew I had found my niche in writing about baseball's Golden Ages and its star players. My website soon began attracting other like-minded baseball history enthusiasts. About three years ago, one such reader, Bill Schaefer, caught my attention. I noticed he was leaving witty, often insightful comments on many of my essays.

As is my custom, I invited Bill to submit a guest essay; and to no great surprise, he accepted the offer. I soon discovered he was no ordinary baseball fan. He possessed an abiding passion for the game along with a deep appreciation for its history. That invitation and the publication of his first essay subsequently led to over 30 such submissions and blossomed into a valued, online friendship. Although we've never met, that friendship has included a lot of good-natured baseball banter over the ensuing years between two ardent fans who happen to share a love for the game and a joy in writing about it.

I learned that Bill is multi-talented with an extensive media background. At various times in his career, he's been a broadcaster, a sports director, a voice-over announcer, and a talk show host. He had interviewed celebrities from the worlds of sports, politics, and entertainment. I was honored that he had chosen my humble website as a vehicle to express his thoughts on baseball history.

I like to think I played a role in helping Bill discover another talent of which he may have been unaware: that of a skilled baseball essayist. I soon recognized his preferred writing style: an engaging, casual tone often laced with personal reflections. When you read Bill's essays, you get the feeling he's talking directly to you. I also loved the way Bill infused his essays with memories of games he attended with his dad. I suggested he continue with this theme. By highlighting the unique father-son bonding experiences that baseball affords its fans, Bill was capturing the very essence of the game's appeal—an appeal that has transcended generations. My hunch was confirmed as his essays soon became a hit with the readers.

In more recent days, I suggested that, with the popularity of his essays, a collection assembled into a single volume might go over well. Bill agreed, and thus was the genesis of this collection of 30 essays of which I'm honored to serve as editor. After a lot of back and forth, trial and error, we settled upon the quirky, slightly off-beat title: *Some Catch: Thirty baseball gems capturing the humor and drama of the game.* It just seemed to be a good fit.

I could cite many passages from Bill's essays demonstrating his clever "way with the written word." Here's just a small sampling:

Rube Waddell:

> "When George Edward Waddell was born October 13, 1876, in Bradford, PA, the cosmos held its breath, with a sense that this was going to be no ordinary human being."

Herman Franks' coaching ability:

> "In early June, Leo Durocher replaced Herman Franks in the third-base coaching box. Franks was so cautious he thought twice before waving a runner around third base on a home run."

The Giants poor start:

> "The club stood 2-12 on April 29. One Giants fan prayed, 'Lord, I asked for a dream season. I'd thank you not to give me a nightmare!'"

Mel Ott:

> "Melvin Thomas Ott let out an ear-splitting scream when he was smacked in the backside a few minutes past 7:00 PM on March 2, 1909, in the family home at Gretna, Louisiana, the product of Charles and Caroline Ott. He was a whopping twelve pounds with a pair of lungs to match his weight."

I love this delightful passage (slightly edited), which I'm quoting at length, from a game he attended with his dad on a blazing hot Sunday afternoon at the Polo Grounds, June 12, 1952. It captures Bill's excellent recall and attention to detail, even for events that took place over 70 years ago. The Giants had erupted for an eleven run lead after three innings. It appeared an easy victory was just ahead for young Bill Schaefer's *Jints*:

> "On this Sunday, my dad and I were at the Polo Grounds to catch a twin bill with those Cardinals. We didn't mind the heat so much but didn't bargain for such a huge crowd precluding us from getting our favorite seats in the upper deck behind home plate...I had consumed one soda and two ice creams by the second inning. It was broiling hot but turning into a wonderful event. Sal Maglie was pitching and the Giants exploded for five runs in the bottom of the second...I was in my glory, never mind the heat, 11-0 at the end of three innings with Sal "The Barber" Maglie on the mound!"

> "Then the gods turned on us. Sal suddenly wilted in the inferno, and got rocked in the fifth inning. St. Loo put up a big SEVEN! Willie Werle came in and shackled the Giants' bats. Hoyt Wilhelm had a rare ragged outing and by the end of seven innings, the score was 11-10. The vendors ran out of refreshments, so I sent

my poor dad out to the concession stand to battle the heat and the mob for soda. He was gone a while and finally made his way down the crowded row juggling two large soda containers. He got jostled and some spilled on his shirt. When he got to me he was livid.

"What happened!" he shouted. I answered meekly, "Solly Hemus just hit a home run into the photographer's ledge in right field (an overhang from the upper deck facade). We're behind 12-11."

"He exploded, *"Don't you EVER send me out for soda pop again!"*

Bill intersperses more than a touch of humor to the essays. Here's a story—one I had never heard—involving the loveable, always quotable, Yogi Berra, whom Bill had also once interviewed:

"Berra was the sweetest guy in the world, and although seldom mistaken for a Rhodes Scholar, he was nothing short of a genius on the field…A radio interviewer once told him before a broadcast, 'We're going to do free association. I'm going to throw out a few names and you just say the first thing that pops into your mind.' Berra agreed."

"On the air the announcer said, 'I'm here tonight with Yogi Berra, and we're going to play free association. I'm going to mention a name and Yogi's just going to say the first thing that comes to mind. Okay, Yogi?' Berra again agreed."

"All right, here we go then. Mickey Mantle."

"What about him?" said Berra.

Readers will enjoy all thirty of Bill's "gems" assembled into this single volume. Some of my favorites include our leadoff essay, "Rube Waddell, the Ultimate Zany." Others of note: "Bill Schaefer's 20 Minutes with Willie Mays (and how he secured a surprise interview with the great star); "Baseball Funny Side Up!" (which received over 10K "likes" when I posted it on my *Old-Time Baseball Photos* Facebook page); and "Baseball's

Contribution to the Lexicon." After rereading many of the essays while preparing this publication, I told Bill I was enjoying them even more on the second reading. Like a fine wine, I told him, they seemed to improve with age.

You also won't want to miss Bill's "Snap Shots of a Giants' Fan Through a Surreal Season," in which Bill recounts the Giants' magical year of 1951. The essay culminates in Bill's account of Bobby Thomson's historic "Shot Heard Round the World." Written from the perspective of a lifelong Giants' fan—and someone who actually has a first-hand recollection of the day— it serves as the centerpiece of the collection.

And so, after a number of years of adding quality baseball content to my website and bringing much joy to my readers, I'm happy to present Bill Schaefer's *Thirty Gems* as a way of paying back this self-proclaimed baseball fanatic. An acknowledged baseball expert and a fine baseball essayist, Bill also happens to be a good friend. I hope you derive as much pleasure from reading it as I had in putting it together.

Gary Livacari
Park Ridge, Illinois
May 2023

RUBE WADDELL: THE ULTIMATE ZANY

"He had more stuff than any pitcher I ever saw"-Connie Mack

"When Waddell had control and some sleep, he was unbeatable."-Branch Rickey

As a young man, he possessed the chiseled features of a matinee idol and developed a penchant for eating animal crackers in bed.

Biographer Alan Levy said: "He was a decidedly different sort of a child." At the age of three, he wandered over to a local fire station and stayed there for several days (much to his parent's consternation). Waddell once left in the middle of a baseball game to go fishing and would delay games to play marbles with kids.

When George Edward Waddell was born October 13, 1876, in Bradford, PA, the cosmos held its breath, with a sense that this was going to be no ordinary human being. He would grow to be powerfully constructed at 6'1", 196 pounds. A jumbo-sized athlete to be sure, when you consider the average male height in the late nineteenth century was less than 5 feet 7 inches tall. George Edward toiled on mining and drilling sites as a kid, which helped his conditioning and arm strength. The nickname "Rube" was bestowed upon him as a natural consequence of his simply looking like a big old country boy.

According to SABR writer, Dan O'Brien,

> "He entered this world on Friday the 13th and exited on April Fools Day. In the 37 intervening years, Rube Waddell struck out more batters, frustrated more managers, and attracted more fans than any pitcher of his era."

He combined charisma, alcoholism, heroic qualities, child-like tendencies, and an extraordinary pitching talent. The Columbus Dispatch wrote,

> "There was a delicious humor in many of his vagaries…an ingenuousness that made them attractive to the public."

He did cartwheels off the mound in victory and once disappeared for months during an off-season, only to be discovered wrestling alligators in a circus. He tried out for the Pittsburgh Pirates in 1897 but was seated next to Manager Patsy Donovan during breakfast and was released immediately after the meal.

However, it was also his pitching talent that made Rube a fan favorite. He threw a heavy fastball and a curve that swooped and darted and may have been the best breaking pitch in the major leagues. Let's look at the record: Over the course of 13 years (1897-1910), Waddell pitched for the Louisville Colonels (NL), Chicago Orphans, Philadelphia Athletics, and St. Louis Browns. The books show a won-lost record of 193-143, with a career ERA of 2.16 (eleventh all-time), 261 complete games, and 50 shutouts. He led the league in ERA twice (1900, 1905), had four consecutive years of 20 or more wins (1902-1905), topped the circuit in strikeouts an amazing six straight years (1902-1907); and in '03 and '04 was the only pitcher to compile consecutive 300-strikeout seasons until Sandy Koufax did it in 1965 and 1966. Waddell's 349 K's in 1904 represented the modern-era major league season record for more than 60 years (sixth on the all-time list) and is still the American League single-season mark for a left-handed pitcher. 1905 saw Waddell win the Triple Crown for pitching with 27 wins, 287 strikeouts and a minuscule 1.48 earned run average.

Rube Waddell was possibly the most eccentric player in the history of the game. According to baseball historian Lee Allen, he began the 1903 season sleeping in a firehouse in Camden NJ and ended it tending bar in a saloon in Wheeling West Virginia. In between, he won 22 games for the Athletics; toured the country in a vaudeville play called *The Stain of Guilt;* got married; saved a woman from drowning; accidentally shot a friend through the hand; and was bitten by a lion. The play was well-received by critics but Waddell's performance was panned royally. He couldn't memorize lines so he was permitted to ad-lib short responses. Nevertheless, his charismatic stage presence drew crowds from far and wide—particularly acclaimed was a scene in which Waddell lifted the actor playing the villain and threw him across the stage with ease. Rube used his sudden stardom to negotiate higher wages for his baseball career (though his highest salary was reported to be a meager $2800).

You'd like to be in the trenches with Rube: In 1904, he carried A's center fielder, Danny Hoffman, knocked unconscious by a fastball to the temple, over his shoulder, on the run across the field…flagged a carriage to a nearby hospital, and thus saved his life.

He also helped save the city of Hickman, Kentucky twice from floods, in 1912 and 1913. Heroically working in icy water for hours led to pneumonia and then tuberculosis, from which he never fully recovered.

Unfortunately, his flakiness and drunken escapades alienated many managers and players, and Rube was shipped to the minor leagues numerous times because of his disruptive tendencies. He was easily distracted by shiny objects held up in the crowd, seemingly mesmerized by them. This could have been a sign of autism, not widely researched back in the day. Only Cornelius Alexander McGillicuddy could tolerate him for any length of time. It paid off for Connie Mack with a Philadelphia A's World Series birth in 1905, mostly due to Waddell's brilliance. (According to SABR, gamblers *may* have bribed Rube, who needed money, to miss the WS against the winning NY Giants). He stayed with "The Tall Tactician" for six years. His battery mate and drinking buddy in Philly was catcher Ossee Schreckengost (Schreck).

My dad used to tell me about Rube Waddell, who ate animal crackers in bed. The story was that his roomie Ossee Schreck was not a happy camper. Here's part of a letter to Connie Mack, purportedly written by Schreck, which appeared in the papers, circa 1906:

> "Dear Connie: This is not a touch for any advance or increase in salary, but something much more serious, and as it won't be long before the Athletics start south for spring practice. I am going to ask you to put Waddell under another charge this year. While I did not mind Rube bringing mocking birds and a reptile or two into our sleeping apartments down south, I do object to his habit of eating crackers in bed…many of them resembling animals. This Rube does nightly.
>
> His crunching of the crackers…the bed was full of crumbs…I would like to suggest that if you can put a clause in his contract that he is not to eat crackers in bed during the 1907 season…we will continue to be real good friends as of yore."

Reports that the request was actually put in the contract might be apocryphal.

Waddell was elected to the HOF in 1946 by the Veterans Committee, looking to enshrine a number of players from his era who had contributed to the growth of the game. Rube drew fans, like a magnet, to ballparks around the country.

Down to 130 pounds from consumption, Waddell passed away on April 1, 1914, in a sanitarium in Elmendorf, Texas. "Dad always had a gleam in his eye when he told stories about Rube Waddell," said Connie Mack's daughter, Ruth Mack Clark. "Dad really loved the Rube."

May 11, 2022

SOURCES: Grunge.com The-true-tragic-story- of- Rube- Waddell; SABR article by Dan O'Brien; Wikipedia, Rube Waddell; Baseball History Daily.com; "Rube and Ossee"; Rube Waddell baseball-reference.

DON MATTINGLY: FAME SECOND TO FAITH AND FAMILY

"A Humble Man of Grace and Dignity. A Captain Who Led by Example. Proud of the Pinstripes Tradition and Dedicated to the Pursuit of Excellence. A Yankee Forever." - Don Mattingly plaque in Monument Park

I loved watching Don Mattingly play baseball. A flawless fielder and an imposing figure in the batter's box: powerful sloping shoulders, intense concentration, with his balanced stance the bat seemingly able to cover every inch of the strike zone. And he was deadly in the clutch, able to rifle a ball to any part of the field with runners on base.

At the turn of the millennium, I had the opportunity to chat with Don in person and on the phone, preparing an article for a local publication. He was a sincere, nice man who liked to get right to the point but was quite forthcoming in his responses. He had been officially retired from active play for about three years, and was a special spring training instructor for the Yankees. He was soon to become an esteemed batting coach for the ball club.

Bill and Mary Mattingly had successfully raised five children in their modest home on the north side of Evansville, Indiana. In addition to daughter Judy, there were four boys, all good athletes. The oldest, Jerry, starred at Rex Mundy High and played basketball at the University of Evansville. Randy was a football hero at Rex and UE, and also a quarterback and punter in the Canadian Football League. Michael played baseball and basketball at the University of Southern Indiana. Donnie, the youngest, led Memorial High in three sports; then rejected a baseball scholarship from Indiana State to sign with the NY Yankees. As Don told me:

> "There was no way I wasn't going to sign with the Yankees and go to college. I never had any misgivings about not attending Indiana State. For some guys college would have been the right choice but, for me, pursuing a career in baseball was absolutely the right decision."

There were mild protestations from dad, Bill, who knew the odds against making the major leagues and wanted his son protected by a college education. But I got the impression it was pretty much a done deal from the start.

The spring of 1979 saw the genesis of Donnie's baseball career, thanks to 27-year-old Jax Robertson, a novice Yankee scout. He had yet to sign anyone who would make it to the majors.

"*Donald Arthur Mattingly, 4/20/61, Evansville* was just one of the names I was running down from my file of player cards in southern Indiana," said

Jax in an interview. He saw Mattingly play just two high school games before advising the Bronx team to draft him, which they eventually did—in the 19th round. With below-average speed, a mediocre arm, and without great power, Don did not possess the tools that attracted baseball scouts. "If I were looking at me as a prospect, I certainly wouldn't have been very impressed," he admitted.

Interestingly, it was a game of "long pepper," which really caught Robertson's attention. It's a game in which the pitcher stands 30 to 40 feet from a hitter, whose job it is to put the head of the bat on the ball. "He was the best pure hitter I'd ever seen," exclaimed the scout. "The most impressive thing about him was the way he manipulated the bat head. The way his hands worked toward the ball. He had that look in his eye, the eye of the tiger."

Don touched on that very thought in assessing what it takes to reach the major leagues—or any goal for that matter:

> "When you look at guys in the minor leagues, whatever level, they're very close in basic skills. The difference is determination and the ability to make adjustments. Also, the player's resolve to stay positive is very important."

Mattingly credits his high school coach, Quentin Merkel, with providing a team prayer that has guided him through life, the essence of which is: *You're in God's hands and if God be with you, who can be against you?* The future manager shared his mind set: "I've always pictured myself having success, being protected in situations. The power of this belief is real and always present."

"The Hit Man" was having a Hall of Fame career when a nagging back problem first reared its ugly head in June of 1987. But through '89 he was still well on track for the Hall. In 1990, the back issue flared and robbed him of his power. But we'll take a look at the macro statistical picture and then specifically at four fantastic years.

SOME CATCH!

Through 14 seasons, Don was on six American League all-star teams, won nine gold gloves, achieved a Most Valuable Player award and captured a batting title. He had a .307 lifetime batting average (higher than Mays, Mantle and Aaron) and totaled a lofty 2153 hits.

But how about '84, '85, '86, '87? Let's review:

- From '85-'87 stroked 96 HR with just 114 strikeouts
- MVP 1985
- Batting Title 1984 (.343)
- RBI Crown 1985 (145)
- Led league in hits twice (broke Earl Combs 1927 club record with 238 in '86
- Led league in doubles three times (broke Gehrig's '27 club record with 53 in '86
- Led league in slugging, OPS, OPS+
- Over the four year span averaged 121 RBI, 211hits, .337 batting average, 155 OPS+
- In 1987, set a then-major league record with six grand slams (Travis Hafner tied in '06)

Without the back ailment Don would have been a shoe-in for a plaque in Cooperstown. On paper he still looks awfully good. Unfortunately, Mattingly dropped off the ballot in 2015. By the way, Donnie Baseball was also ambidextrous, having actually played in a game in 1983, as a left-handed second baseman, and in three games as a left handed third baseman, in 1986!

I asked Don why he was so good in pressure situations.

> "I grew up in a competitive atmosphere with my brothers and through the years it was preparation and concentration. Even in batting practice I tried to hit every good pitch hard. This carried over to game situations. I just enjoyed playing."

In 1995, the Yankees, like *Gigi* in Alan Jay Lerner's Best Movie musical, were "trembling on the brink." They simply could not handle the Mariners in Seattle. It was the Captain's final year and he influenced many of the players who would carry the Bronx Bombers to three World Championships to close out the millennium. Paul O'Neil credits Don with helping him enormously with the New York media. Bernie Williams, Mike Stanley, and Derek Jeter all had words of praise, with Jeter saying, "He led by example, regardless of what happened."

Many feel Mattingly quit because of his recurring back issues, curtailing his power production, and that he would never be the hitter he was half a dozen years earlier. I wondered, had he put together a great year in '95, might he have continued?

> "No, I would have retired anyway. On the road that year, increasingly, my thoughts were constantly of wanting to be home. My heart wasn't in the game-I just longed to be with my wife and kids in Indiana."

Ironically, Don said he thought he'd regained his power stroke in late '95 and believed he could have pounded out some strong numbers the following year. He certainly finished with a flourish, batting .417 in the divisional series with a spate of ribbies and a dramatic home run.

At the age of 50, Donald Arthur Mattingly began his managerial career in 2011, for the Los Angeles Dodgers. He replaced the just-retired Joe Torre, his former manager. For five years he guided the Dodgers to three consecutive National League West division titles, finished second for National League Manager of the Year in 2013, and led his team to a nifty .551 winning pct. (446-363). Clayton Kershaw summed up the players feelings about their manager, "He's so positive. All he asks of us is just go out there and play the way we're supposed to. When it's that simple, it's easy and fun to play."

As of this writing, June is bustin' out all over for Mattingly and the Marlins, as Miami is firmly ensconced in second place in the National

League East. Shades of the bizarre 2020 season when Donny Baseball piloted his club to a stunning playoff berth and won National League Manager of the Year? We hope Don sticks around awhile.

Twenty-one years ago, Don told me he wouldn't be shattered if he were not inducted into the Hal of Fame:

> "All the fame I need in this lifetime occurred on August 31, 1997 when my number 23 was retired in ceremonies at Yankee Stadium. It was like a dream that day…I felt like a kid again… looking out at number 3, number 4, number 5, number 7. All those great players and to have my number retired with them."

Any regrets, I asked?

> "No regrets. Oh, there's a tingle inside when I consider all those World Series rings I missed out on. But when I weigh it against all the blessings I have with my family and the moments I've been able to share with them, it's not even close."

I have a hunch his answer would be pretty much the same today.

January 13, 2021

BILL SCHAEFER'S TWENTY MINUTES WITH WILLIE MAYS

"He can hit. He can run. He can field...If he could cook, I'd marry him!" - Leo Durocher, speaking of Willie Mays

On May 11, 1972, the Mets made a trade with the San Francisco Giants to acquire Willie Mays for pitcher Charlie Williams and $50,000. The baseball legend had just recently celebrated his 41st birthday. The innocent, effervescent "Say Hey Kid" who turned the New York Giants Baseball Nation on its collective ear 21 years earlier, had belted 646 of his 660 total career homers. But maybe he still had enough left to help his new team recapture their own recent glory.

I was wearing many broadcasting hats for local radio station WJDM in Elizabeth, NJ at the time, and thought it would be cool if I could do a live phone interview with Mays on my Saturday music show, on June third. The Mets would be home for a couple of weeks, so why not? Well, logically, there were a few "why nots." First, Willie never heard of a local announcer named Bill Schaefer. Second, he never heard of the little 500-watt radio station in north-central New Jersey.

The third was a little more complicated. Mays loved everybody when he first joined the New York Giants in late May of 1951. And everybody instantly loved him. Despite a slow start at the plate, fans just knew instinctively Mays possessed Leo Durocher's five tools of a great player (hit, hit with power, run, throw, and field). But, as the Giants manager so perfectly put it, "He had the other magic ingredient that turns a superstar into a super Superstar - charisma. He lit up a room when he came in. He was a joy to be around."

Then a funny thing happened when the Giants moved to the left coast in 1958 and opened the season at Seals Stadium. The fans didn't take to the star the way they did in New York. Perhaps some of the older fans still had an allegiance to the beloved Joe DiMaggio who patrolled center field in the same spacious ballpark, with ease and brilliance, in 1935. Others may have felt a player from a big east coast city was something of an outlier, and not one of their own. They considered rookie phenom Orlando Cepeda more of a homegrown product and showered him with the affection Mays was used to receiving.

This hurt Willie. And he began to develop a small chip on his shoulder, which grew in the years to come. The Baby Bull became a great player and was Rookie of the Year in 1958. But Mays concentrated on his hitting and achieved his highest career batting average of .347 (barely losing the batting crown on the last day of the season to Richie Ashburn's .350). Mays also led the league in runs scored (121), stolen bases with 31 (84% success), and OPS+ (165). He fielded like no other. But the fans were slow to come around.

Mays encountered turbulence in his career and personal life through the '60s and matured as a fine leader. But he also became guarded, harboring a touch of bitterness. By the time he joined the Mets, he was generally cool to the press and not inclined to give lengthy interviews. I was aware of most of this at the time but plowed ahead anyway. My first step was to call the Mets directly to find the club's hotel headquarters. I stated my case: Sports Director for WJDM; our audience loves the Mets and Willie Mays; we want to welcome him back to NY with a live phone interview. No problem. Nice as could be. I was given the hotel phone number and immediately called their front desk.

Again, the gentleman I reached couldn't have been more cooperative. So, I said, "Great, I'll call the hotel a little after 10 am Saturday, and you'll put me through to Willie Mays' room for the interview, OK?" The clerk replied, "Yes, call then and we'll put you right through." All this was done with an assumptive attitude, mind you, like "no" was not an option. Oh, the boldness of youth!

Like clockwork, I called the hotel on Saturday, shortly after the news at 10, and, bang, zoom, I was suddenly talking to perhaps the greatest player of all time! Stifling an instant case of nerves, I introduced myself and thanked him for coming on for a phone interview (which he didn't even know about!). The biggest thing I had going for me was the element of surprise. Mays was slightly bewildered and I started asking questions right and left. Twenty minutes later Mays abruptly said, "Hey man, you writin' a book!" I forced a chuckle and blurted out, "Well, I'm a big fan of yours, Willie." He didn't have to hit me over the head, the interview was over. I thanked him profusely and got out of there. Our small but loyal audience loved it. WJDM General Manager, Harry Anger, said, "Very enterprising." That was in lieu of money, of course...

The surreal event reminded me of the classic 1979 movie, *Being There*. Peter Sellers had created the unforgettable character, Chauncey Gardener (Chance), who, in the final scene, walks on water. There was nothing spiritual about it. The simple-minded Chance simply did not know the laws of physics wouldn't allow a creature of Earth to walk on water. I did not think for one split second that I would not have an interview with Willie Mays.

Emboldened, I executed the same plan with, Rusty Staub, the following Saturday. He answered groggily and was barely coherent. After four minutes of mumbled answers, I politely ended the interview. I have a hunch "Le Grande Orange" had a few choice words for the front desk later that day!

If you haven't already, please read [Gary Livacari's perfect 90th Birthday Tribute to Willie Mays](), which appeared on the website, May 6th.

June 29, 2021

BASEBALL APPETIZERS FOR THE '21 SEASON

Say this much for Baseball--it is beyond question the greatest conversation piece ever invented in America -Bruce Catton

Statistics are used like a drunk uses a lamppost—for support not illumination - Vin Scully

We love to think about baseball and talk baseball and figure out how our favorite team is going to do this year. Like we did as kids, we still want to believe the players play the game for the sheer joy of playing and not so much for the money. We want them to run hard to first base on every ground ball. We don't need super statistical compilations to tell us what batter is a good bet to get a clutch hit and what pitcher will get a big out when the game is on the line. And we hope someone will tell the baseball manufacturers that we don't want a batted ball to take off like a 2-iron shot in the fairway of Augusta National Golf Club.

Most of us can't wait for the baseball season to start with real people in the stands again and a full season to enjoy. But now let's go back in time, as I share an amazing baseball game experience and a few lovable Larry Berra items.

The Nightmare at Coogan's Bluff

It was a blazing hot Sunday, June 15, 1952, at the Polo Grounds. The sun was shining mercilessly, with the thermometer popping at 97 degrees. The Giants were playing good ball with a record of 32-17, four games behind the Dodgers in second place. The club was coming off their miracle pennant run of '51, but was not the same at its core. Willie Mays had departed for military service in May, Monte Irvin suffered a broken ankle in spring training and would be out until mid-August, and spark plug Eddie Stanky was traded to the St. Louis Cardinals to become their player/manager.

On this Sunday, my dad and I were at the Polo Grounds to catch a twin bill with those Cardinals. We didn't mind the heat so much, but the huge crowd drove us far from our favorite seats in the upper deck, behind home plate. We had to settle for deep second deck seats way out in left-center field, at almost the curve of the huge horseshoe configuration. The vendors were in top form ("Hey, cold soda here!" "Hey, ice cream here!"). I had consumed one soda and two ice creams by the second inning. It was broiling hot but turning into a wonderful event. Sal Maglie was pitching and the Giants exploded for five runs in the bottom of the second. A Cardinal fan was seated right behind me. He was about 35 and a pleasant, friendly man. In the third inning, the Cards brought in a relief pitcher named Jack Crimean. I remembered him from earlier in the year. He stunk on ice and I was laughing it up, really giving it to the Cardinal fan. Sure enough, Crimean got creamed—to the tune of six runs, seven hits (two homers) and a walk. I was in my glory, never mind the heat--11-0 at the end of three innings with Sal "The Barber" Maglie on the mound!

Then the gods turned on us. Sal suddenly wilted in the inferno, and got rocked in the fifth inning. St. Loo put up a big SEVEN! Willie Werle came in and shackled the Giants' bats. Hoyt Wilhelm had a rare ragged outing and by the end of seven innings, the score was 11-10. The vendors ran out of refreshments, so I sent my poor dad out to the concession stand to battle the heat and the mob for soda. He was gone a while and finally made his way down the crowded row juggling two large soda containers. He got jostled and some spilled on his shirt. When he got to me he was livid, "What happened!" he shouted. I answered meekly, "Solly Hemus just hit a home run into the photographer's ledge in right field (an overhang from the upper deck facade). We're behind 12-11."

He exploded, "Don't you EVER send me out for soda pop again!"

The Giants lost 14-12. I begged my dad to leave so we could catch a movie on 42nd street. He was adamant, "I never walked out on a game in my life!" The Giants won the nightcap 3-0 on a three-run clout by Wes Westrum, behind Dave Koslo. The contest was called because of a Sunday curfew after seven innings. But nothing could numb the pain of that first game.

YOGI NEVER GETS OLD

In March 1970, I was the Sports Director of a new radio station in Elizabeth NJ. The GM thought it would be nice if I called the Mets spring training headquarters in St. Petersburg, Fla, and get coach Yogi Berra on the phone to give us a brief promo for the brand new station.

Yogi was on the line in a jiffy. I stated my name and affiliation and what we'd like him to do in the way of a promo message. He was incredibly nice. I said, "Yogi, Just say, 'Hi, this is Yogi Berra. I'd like to welcome a new station to the metropolitan area-WJDM, Elizabeth, NJ.'" After three tries he gave up, "Jeez, Bill, I just can't get it." I apologized for not providing a written copy for the promo, shortened it a tad, and we were good.

Berra was the sweetest guy in the world, and although seldom mistaken for a Rhodes Scholar, he was nothing short of a genius on the field. Yogi handled pitchers and defensive alignments brilliantly. So well, in fact, that Casey Stengel used to introduce him as "Mr. Berra, which is my assistant manager."

"I didn't say everything I said," Yogi once insisted, but the following are verifiably on the record:

A radio interviewer once told him before a broadcast, "We're going to do free association. I'm going to throw out a few names and you just say the first thing that pops into your mind." Berra agreed.

On the air the announcer said, "I'm here tonight with Yogi Berra, and we're going to play free association. I'm going to mention a name and Yogi's just going to say the first thing that comes to mind. Okay, Yogi?" Berra again agreed.

"All right, here we go then. Mickey Mantle."

"What about him?" said Berra.

Many Yogi stories involve his attachment to comic books. But when his teammates chided him about his addiction to comics, he answered shrewdly, "If that's so silly, how come every time I put one down, somebody else picks it up?"

Rogers Hornsby had this to say about the long off-season, "People ask me what I do in winter when there's no baseball. I'll tell you what I do. I stare out the window and wait for spring."

Well, spring is finally here. Are we ready?

March 28, 2021

Sources: 1952 Giants/Cardinals Roster; 1952 Giants schedule almanac; 1952 NL standing of the clubs, June 14; 1952 box score Giants/Cardinals, June 15; The Bathroom Baseball Book, Red-Letter Press, INC., Saddle River, NJ.; Baseball Anecdotes, Daniel Okrent-Steve Wulf, Oxford University Press, 1989; The Wit & Wisdom of Baseball, Saul Wisnia with Dan Schlossberg, 2007 Publications International, Ltd.; 100 best baseball quotes, internet google search.

TRAGIC STORY OF BASEBALL'S UNFORTUNATE HALL-OF-FAMER, ERNIE LOMBARDI

The Yankees break open a 4-4, tenth-inning tie in Game Four of the World Series when Joe DiMaggio slides past Cincinnati catcher Ernie Lombardi—still recovering from a collision with Charlie Keller seconds earlier—to give the Yankees a three-run lead and, half an inning later, their fourth straight world title.

"Next to Ernie molasses is a blur"–Anonymous teammate

"Lombardi was so slow he ran like he was carrying a piano—and the tuner"-Anonymous teammate

Although Ernesto Natali Lombardi would probably have lost a race to a snail, he pulverized baseballs, winding up with a .306 career batting average spanning 17 years, with an overlapping golf club batting grip. Pretty good, since he seldom beat out an infield hit. I was intrigued by him as a kid because my dad told me he once saw Lombardi thrown out from short left field on an apparent line-drive single. This is why I'm adding my two cents about the big backstop, following webmaster Gary

Livacari's outstanding essay, from earlier this year, focusing on Ernie's alleged World Series gaffe.

Ernie played with the Brooklyn Robins, Reds, Braves, and Giants, beginning his career in 1931(the year Las Vegas legalized gambling) and playing his last year with New York in 1947 (the year transistors and the mobile phone were invented). I was a red-hot "hang-on-every-pitch" Giants fan when Lombardi belted four circuit shots that year, contributing to the team's then-record 221 home runs.

The Schnozz

At 6' 3" 230 pounds Ernie was huge, especially for a catcher, with a nose to match. "The Schnozz" moniker was a perfect fit with his prominent proboscis. Asked if the players and coaches razzed him about his oversized honker, Ernie answered good-naturedly, "No. It was mostly the fans in Oakland before I got to the majors who started calling me 'Schnozz'."

An excellent signal-caller, Lombardi was adored by his pitchers, particularly Johnny Vander Meer. They were Cincinnati battery mates for both of Vander Meer's consecutive no-hitters, June 11 and 15, 1938. The first, at Crosley Field against the Boston Bees, went into the books as a 3-0 win for the left-hander, with a tremendous assist from Lombardi. He walloped a key homer and unloaded two rifle throws to first nailing two base runners. "Lom would pick off six or seven guys a year throwing side-arm behind left-handed hitters," said the appreciative Vander Meer.

The second no-hit whitewash, 6-0, took place at Ebbets Field. It was the first night game at the Brooklyn ball field, and in New York City. This one was tougher, as Johnny walked eight and left the bags loaded in the ninth. Home plate umpire Bill Stewart observed,

SOME CATCH!

"Sure, Vander Meer had to pitch perfectly to get his no-hitters, but give some credit to Lombardi. His judgment in calling pitches was just as perfect and just as important."

The two other Cincinnati aces, Bucky Walters and Paul Derringer, had impeccable command, "You could sit in a rocking chair and catch them guys," said Ernie. But Johnny V. was more erratic and once uncorked a pitch way outside. Lombardi reached for the ball with his bare hand and snagged it. As Vander Meer later exclaimed:

"Listen, if you're going to sit back there and catch me bare-handed, the least you could do is shake your hand a little like I had something on the pitch. You're making me look bad!"

Lombardi possessed huge blacksmith mitts and could hold seven baseballs in one hand (Johnny Bench could also do this). Remarkably agile around the plate and possessing a cannon for an arm, he led the National League in putouts, double plays and caught stealing percentage, one season apiece. He had four consecutive years ('35- '38) where he batted a composite .338. Taking all the great hitting catchers, including Piazza, Mauer, Dickey, Hartnett, Cochrane, Bench, Berra, Fiske, Campanella—only Mike Piazza at .343, had a four year run with a higher batting average. The Schnozz won the batting crown in 1938 (.342), along with an MVP. And he won another title in 1942 (.330).

As so articulately expressed in Gary Livacari's piece, Ernie Lombardi was vilified unnecessarily by the press because of an incident on October 8, 1939, in Game Four of the Yankees vs. Reds World Series. The Yanks were dominating three-games-to-none and looked to sweep with the score tied 4-4 in the tenth inning. Joe DiMaggio singled home the tie-breaking run, with Charlie Keller also trying to score and plowing into Lom, knocking him into a daze, as he safely crossed the plate. DiMag also scored, as the prostrate catcher was unable to offer more than a feeble swipe at the Yankee Clipper, scoring the final run of the World Series.

But "King Kong" Keller, at the next spring training, denied even touching Lombardi. Johnny Vander Meer had this take:

"Ival Goodman's throw from right field short-hopped Lom and caught him in the groin and paralyzed him. Anybody but Lombardi they would have had to carry him off the field."

A bum rap indeed was "Lombardi's Big Snooze," as the crazy play had nothing whatever to do with the outcome of the series. And further amplification revealed that for some unknown reason Lom was not wearing a protective cup at the time.

> "Be kind, for everyone you meet is fighting a harder battle."-Plato

Ernie never got over the terrible "Big Snooze" reference and being denied by the writers a place in the Hall of Fame. He fell into depression later in his life and agreed to get help. But while visiting relatives he excused himself to visit the bathroom and didn't return. His wife found him in the bedroom with his throat slashed by a razor. Fortunately, medics arrived and saved his life. Ernie passed away in 1977 after a long illness. He was loved by the fans, by all accounts a terrific teammate and an amiable giant - but died a bitter man.

Fortunately, Birdie Tebbetts, a fine catcher in his own right, became a member of the Veterans Committee and almost single-handedly pushed Lombardi through for election into The Hall, posthumously, in 1986.

October 3, 2022

Sources: Baseball Reference.com; Ernie Lombardi, Wikipedia; Plato's quotations.com; Ernie Lombardi quotes.com; SABR Bioproject: article, Joseph Wancho.

BASEBALL'S CUTTING EDGE HUMOR: *"THE GLORY OF THEIR (FUNNY) LINES"*

"In our sun-down perambulations of late, through the outer parts of Brooklyn, we have observed several parties of youngsters playing "base," a certain game of ball…Let us go forth awhile, and get better air in our lungs. Let us leave our close rooms…The game of ball is glorious."-- *Walt Whitman, 1846*

Few can turn a phrase like Whitman. Baseball certainly can be glorious but it also possesses the key element of cutting-edge humor. Rafael Sabitini's novel, *Scaramouche*, opens with the memorable line, "He was born with a gift of laughter and a sense that the world was mad." A British actor once said, "In an altogether unreasonable world, laughter is the emergency exit for humans."

In preparing the essay, it was a real labor of love—becoming immersed in the funny, sometimes profound quotes running the gamut of baseball people and including some of the all-time characters of the game. The only thing missing for me was the intoxicating aroma of cigar smoke, which permeated the Polo Grounds and Yankee Stadium back in the day. (Unfortunately, my wife stopped smoking her Cuban corona imports shortly after we got married).

Let's enter into baseball's unique lexicon and see what we've got…

"Baseball is reassuring. It makes me feel as if the world isn't going to blow up."—Sharon Olds.

"Say this much for big league baseball—it is beyond any question the greatest conversation piece ever invented in America."—Bruce Catton

"He hits from both sides of the plate. He's amphibious."—Yogi Berra

"All I can tell 'em is I pick out a good one and sock it. I get back to the dugout and they ask me what it was I hit and I tell 'em I don't know except it looked good."—Babe Ruth

"So I'm ugly. So what? I never saw anyone hit with his face."—Lawrence Peter Berra

"I can remember a reporter asking for a quote, and I didn't know what a quote was. I thought it was some kind of soft drink."—Joe DiMaggio

"I became a good pitcher when I stopped trying to make them miss the ball and started trying to make them hit it."—Sandy Koufax

"You can sum up the game of baseball in one word: you never know."—Joaquin Andujar.

"I never took the game home with me. I always left it in some bar."—Bob Lemon

"Winning is the most important thing in my life, after breathing. Breathing first, winning next."—George Steinbrenner

SOME CATCH!

"It ain't nothin' till I call it."—legendary umpire, Bill Klem

"They broke it to me gently. The manager came up to me before a game and told me they didn't allow visitors in the clubhouse."—Bob Uecker

"I knew my career was over. In 1965, my baseball card came out with no picture."—Bob Uecker

Wait There's More...

"I never questioned the integrity of an umpire. Their eyesight, yes."-Leo Durocher

"They give you a round bat and they throw you a round ball. And they tell you to hit it square."—Willie Stargell

"If horses won't eat it (artificial turf), I don't want to play on it."—Dick Allen

"If you get three strikes, not even the best lawyer in the world can get you off."-Bill Veeck (as in wreck)

"All I remember about my wedding day in 1967, is that the Cubs lost a doubleheader."—George Will

"A lot of people my age are dead at the present time."—Casey Stengel

"I don't want to play golf. When I hit the ball I want others to chase it."—Rogers Hornsby

"Rooting for the Yankees is like rooting for the house in blackjack."—Adam Morrow

"If you don't think too good, don't think too much."—Ted Williams

"I'd rather be the shortest player in the majors than the tallest player in the minors."—Freddie Patek (nicknamed The Flea, shortstop Patek was the smallest MLB player of his time at 5'5").

"Slumps are like a soft bed. They're easy to get into and hard to get out of."—Johnny Bench

Rounding Third—Can We Beat the Throw?

"Ninety feet between the bases is the nearest thing to perfection that man has yet achieved."—Red Smith

"On Father's Day, we again wish you all a happy birthday."—Ralph Kiner

"If God let you hit a home run last time up, then who struck you out the time before that?"—Sparky Anderson

"My goals are to hit .300, score 100 runs, and stay injury prone."—Mickey Rivers

"This is really more fun than being president. I really do love baseball and I wish we could do this out on the lawn every day."—Ronald Reagan on playing ball with old-timers, 1983

"Baseball is only a game, but they keep a book on you. When it's all over for you, the game has got you measured."—Joe Garagiola

"Gimme good pitching and long hitting, and let the rest of them managers get just as smart as they want!"—manager Wilbert Robinson

"Don't pull that stuff on me. How can a pipsqueak like you be Babe Ruth's manager?"—doorman to diminutive Yankees skipper Miller Huggins

"Throw strikes. The plate don't move."—Satchel Paige

"Josh, I wish you and Satchel played with me on the Cardinals. Hell, we'd win the pennant by July 4 and go fishin' until World Series time."—Dizzy Dean to Josh Gibson in 1934

"Above anything else, I hate to lose."—Jackie Robinson

"Son, I won more games than you'll ever see."—Cy Young, to a young reporter

"With this batting slump I'm in, I was so happy to hit a double that I did a tap dance on second base. They tagged me between taps."—Frenchy Bordagaray

A Jolley Ending!

We'll close with this funny story concerning Smead Jolley, who so fit his name in looks and personality. Big for his era at 6'3", 210, Jolley was gregarious and confident and batted .367 in 16 minor league seasons. For four years in the majors (1930-33), with the White Sox and Red Sox, he hit .305 with good power. But Smead was an intensely bad fielder. In his rookie year with Chicago, Jolley was tutored extensively by manager Donie Bush on how to run up the sloping hill, then known as "Duffy's Cliff," which fronted the 37-foot wall at Fenway Park. Smead navigated the slope well on May 22, but ran into trouble the next day. Running up the hill on a fly ball, a sudden gust of wind buffeted the drive. Jolley stopped and dove from the top of the incline, skidding on his chin all the way down. The ball bounced off his head. The crowd howled hysterically. Smead didn't think it was so funny, "Donie taught me how to go up the slope but didn't teach me how to come down!"

September 18, 2022

Sources: Baseball, an Illustrated History, Geoffrey C. Ward and Ken Burns; Rafael Sabitini, Wikipedia; SABR, article Smead Jolley, by Bill Nowlin; 2715 One-Line Quotations for Speakers, Writes and Raconteurs, Edward F. Murphy; The Wit & Wisdom of Baseball, Saul Wisnia with Dan Schlossberg; The Bathroom Baseball Book, Red-Letter Press, Inc.; Smead Jolley, baseball reference, web.

THE STRANGE CASE OF VON McDANIEL

"All the bright precious things fade so fast—and they don't come back."
The Great Gatsby

"[Von McDaniel] was an instant major league pitching sensation in 1957, a struggling Class B hurler in 1958, and a career minor league infielder by 1959." -Unknown sportswriter

As World War II sunk its teeth into Eastern Europe in 1939, worlds away in the tiny southwestern town of Hollis Oklahoma, on April 18, Newell and Ada Mae McDaniel were blessed with the middle of their three sons, Max Von McDaniel. Tenant farmers, the McDaniels survived The Great Depression and raised their children to follow the teachings of the Good Book. Seldom was any family member seen without a bible.

Older brother Lindy McDaniel was signed at 19 as a $50,000 "bonus baby" by the St. Louis Cardinals in 1955 and carved himself a fine 21-year career. Initially a starter, he became a premier relief pitcher for the Cards, Cubs, Giants, Yankees, and Royals. Lindy played with more than 300 teammates and pitched for eight different managers. Throwing a monster curve and a diving forkball, McDaniel was named The National League Sporting News Reliever of the Year twice.

THE METEORIC RISE OF VON McDANIEL

At age 18, Von McDaniel was considered a better pitching prospect than his older brother. A lean 180 pounds well-proportioned over a 6' 2" frame gave Von the look of an athlete. An all-state basketball star, he rejected a scholarship to Kansas University because his dream was to pitch for the St. Louis Cardinals—with his brother Lindy.

In his three years pitching for Arnett High School, Von hurled 243 innings, allowing only 25 hits. Hardly anyone got on base, so he had to receive special instruction on how to pitch from a stretch! He also batted .545.

All 16 Major League teams pursued him and many offered more than the $50,000 bonus given to Lindy. But his dad, Newell, was adamant, "Von will accept exactly what Lindy got, not a penny more or a penny less!" On May 23, 1957, just four days after graduating as class valedictorian, Von McDaniel signed a bonus contract for 50K, requiring him to start his career in the majors with the Cardinals. Three weeks later on June 13, barely 18, Von blanked the Phillies for four innings in a mop-up role, allowing only a single hit.

A few days later, the rookie entered a tie game at Ebbets Field and was about to face "The Duke of Flatbush," Duke Snider. Shortstop Alvin Dark made a beeline for the mound to alert his kid pitcher, "You know who this is, Von?" The youngster's reply was confident but respectful, "Oh sure. That's Mr. Snider." McDaniel then proceeded to fan the future

Hall-of-Famer on five pitches. Von duplicated his previous performance with four scoreless innings of one-hit ball, resulting in his first win. The Duke enthused, "He's real good...a fine curveball and exceptional control."

On June 21, the young phenom made his first major league start at Busch Stadium against the same Brooklyn Dodgers and recorded a brilliant two-hit shutout. Another win at home against the Phillies gave him a 3-0 record for the month of June.

A couple of losses in July were bookended by a pair of sensational outings. On July second, Von took a perfect game into the seventh inning and topped the great Warren Spahn, 4-2, at Milwaukee's County Stadium. Twenty-six days later, on a hazy, humid afternoon in St. Louis, Von faced the Pittsburgh Pirates in the first game of a doubleheader. It was his best game - a dazzling one-hit whitewash, retiring the first 22 batters he faced! He was now 5-2 heading into August and major league owners were drooling. They would enjoy a 20-percent increase in attendance when the teenager pitched, home or away.

Von McDaniel was an adorable wunderkind, with a wholesome country boy look. My best friend's grandmother, effecting an unintentional yet perfect imitation of radio/ TV icon, Molly Goldberg, said, "Nice looking boy. Clean and cut." He was also part of an emerging brother pitching act. During the summer of 1957, Lindy and Von were featured in *Sports Illustrated, Time, Newsweek,* and *Life*. Each compared them to the legendary duo of Dizzy and Paul Dean. "These fellas are going a long way," predicted Dizzy Dean. "One day they'll sure enough win 49 games in a season like me and Paul did."

Unfortunately, Von won only two more games in the big leagues. His final victory was an impressive route-going performance against the Giants at the Polo Grounds, 3-2, on August 20 (Von's major league log was 7-5, with a 3.45 ERA, ironically the same as his brother Lindy!)

THE METEORIC DESCENT

Actually, the first signs of erosion were evident that September of '57. Von made two starts pitching only 3.1 innings. He yielded eight hits, seven runs, two homers, and walked six batters. Cooperstown inductee, Warren Spahn, offered a cogent comment, "A young pitcher breaking into the big leagues must have the good fastball and he must show it to the hitters. Von is 18…and pitching like an old man."

Fearing too much pressure on a young arm, the St. Louis brain trust told their precious talent to rest up for the coming 1958 season. The following spring training was a disaster. Von couldn't find the plate and couldn't dent a cream puff with his fastball. And it got worse when the season opened. Pitching in two games, he threw just two innings, yielding five hits, five walks, and three runs. As Von later admitted:

"I did not take care of myself in the winter months. I was weak the next spring training. I had no power in my arm and I messed up my delivery by trying too hard. Then I injured the long muscle in my back. Also, I'd grown another inch and gained 10 pounds, which didn't help."

On May 14, McDaniel was optioned to Double-A Houston where he yielded 29 runs in 18 innings of work. Manager Harry Walker thought it was a problem of overthinking on the mound and using too much wrist in his delivery. Demoted again, Von found himself with Class-B Winston Salem. Skipper Vern Benson had this assessment, "There is no rhythm at all in his pitching motion. He throws like a girl who has never picked up a baseball." This virtually marked the end of Von McDaniel's pitching career at the tender age of 20. He would never return to the big leagues.

Sinking deeper into the minors, Von started the 1959 season with the Daytona Beach Islanders, in the Class-D Florida State League—but this time as the starting shortstop. Through the next eight years, mostly as an infielder, he bounced between Double and Triple-A, compiling a .255 minor league batting average. He retired after the 1966 season.

Von was not displeased with his fate. He was happily married with four daughters, working as a farmer, accountant, and part-time preacher. He left us too soon, succumbing to heart issues at the age of 56, in 1995.

The former "Mr. Von-derful" enjoyed his life and offered this comment,

"I was just real excited to be playing ball. Playing in the major leagues was fine, but just playing pro baseball was enough. I think I proved my point that I could play, by sticking around for 10 years."

So let's take a moment to shine our baseball spotlight on Von McDaniel, a fine pitcher with an abundance of talent and plenty of promise. Unfortunately, Von joins the ranks of the many ballplayers who, for one reason or another, never really achieved lasting success in the Big Show.

May 11, 2021

Sources: Baseball reference.com Cardinals schedule almanac, '57, '58; Oklahoman.com/article/1983/Bob Hersom; Von McDaniel/SABR/article/David E. Skelton; Lindy and Von McDaniel, Wikipedia pages

BASEBALL, FUNNY SIDE UP!

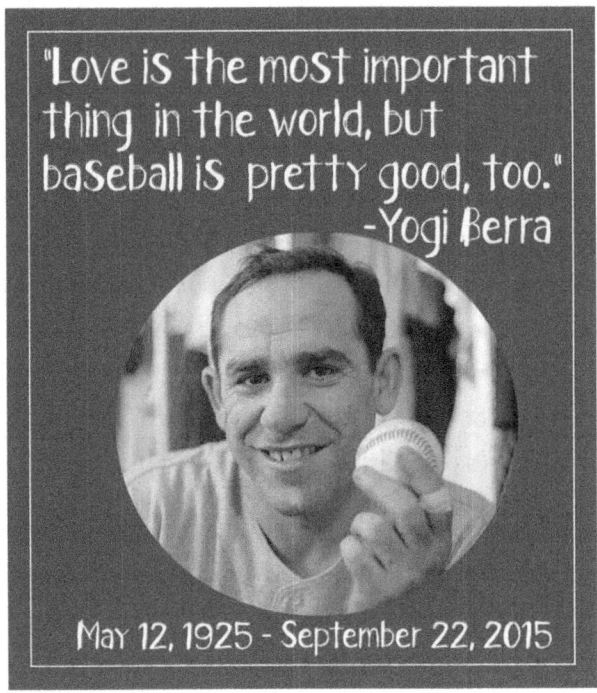

The funniest and strangest material on earth can be found in the archives of baseball's stories, wisdom, and hilarious impromptu comments. Though at times sans the king's English, nobody can write it better than just quoting the people associated with our great game. With your permission, we'll delve into those vaults of one-liners and offbeat stories.

Freddie Hutchinson, a fine pitcher for the Detroit Tigers and well-respected manager of the Tigers, Cardinals, and Reds, seldom smiled. Once, noticing his perennially dour expression, a reporter asked Hutch why he always sported a sour puss. Hutchinson, bouncing off a Joe Garagiola line, replied, "I'm really happy, my face just don't know it,"

Ralph Kiner, revered Hall-of-Fame slugger and beloved broadcaster for the New York Mets came up with some dandies over the years, known as "Kinerisms." He once opened his post-game show with, "Hello everybody, welcome to Kiner's Korner, this is Ralph Korner." He also said, "Now up to bat for the New York Mets is Gary Cooper (he meant Gary Carter). And then there was, "We'll be back after this word from Manufacturers Hangover."

On a personal note, Kiner used to drive me nuts by misquoting the great Gas House Gang and New York Giant second baseman, Frankie Frisch. For years, he would refer to Frankie Frisch's famous line and say "Oh, them bases on balls." He thus portrayed Frisch as a sparsely educated old-timer, but with keen insight. "The Fordham Flash" was actually an articulate college grad who did the Giants' radio broadcasts with Steve Ellis in 1947 and '48, between managerial stints. They finally corrected Ralph (Oh, *those* bases on balls) and I found it in my heart to forgive him.

I chatted with Yogi Berra on the phone during spring training in 1970 and got a colorful promo for a new AM radio station in Elizabeth, NJ, WJDM 1530. Nicest man in the world. We'll get to a funny story about Yogi later in the essay. But two Berra Beauties stand out for me: On a hot humid day, Berra was attending a ceremony where New York mayor, John Lindsay, was presenting him with the key to the city. The mayor's wife, Mary, remarked, "My, how cool you look." Yogi replied, "And you don't look so hot yourself." (Berra confirmed this in his 1998 "The Yogi Book" but varying versions of the joke actually go back to 1934), Then there was a reference to a popular restaurant in The Hill section of St. Louis. Yogi's comment was, "Nobody goes there anymore. It's too crowded." You can't beat that logic.

Lefty Gomez pitched in five World Series and is honored in Cooperstown. And no one had a sharper sense of humor. To wit: a reporter asked "El Goofo" if he would throw at his own mother. "You're damn right I would," blurted Lefty, "she's a good hitter." He said, "When Neil Armstrong first set foot on the moon, he and all the space scientists were puzzled by an unidentifiable white object; I knew immediately what it was…that was a home run ball hit off me in 1933 by Jimmie Foxx." He also revealed, "The secret of my success is clean living and a fast outfield."

How about Dizzy Dean and Satchel Paige? Let's jump in. Diz remarked, "It ain't braggin' if you can back it up." And, "The good Lord was good to me. He gave me a strong body, a good right arm, and a weak mind." He once said, "Son, what kind of pitch do you want to miss?"

Ole Satch had this advice, "Don't look back, something might be gaining on you." On another occasion, he opined, "Avoid fried foods, which angry up the blood." Then he offered, "Sometimes I sits and thinks and sometimes I just sits." Finally, "I don't know what you're going to do, Mr. Dean. But I'm not going to give up any runs if we have to stay here all night."

Here are a few stories I think you'll enjoy.

Most baseball historians consider the first major league season to have been 1876, when the Chicago White Stockings were the founding members of the new National League. The pitchers stood 50 feet from home plate and threw underhand. The batter could call for a high or a low ball and then "strike" the ball, as in Cricket. One of the great stars was a smallish second baseman named Ross Barnes. The dapper 145-pounder took full advantage of the rules at the time, which counted any batted ball that struck first in fair territory as a fair ball, regardless of where it ultimately settled. His specialty was chopping at a pitched ball so that it hit in front of the plate and then caromed into foul territory. Barnes sent infielders into a tizzy, chasing the crazily spinning spheroids into the distant reaches beyond the foul lines! Barnes batted .429 that year and scored 126 runs in just 66 games. The rules were changed the next year and Barnes became seriously ill, never to become an offensive force again.

Yogi Berra was said to be notorious for borrowing the contents of shaving kits left on the sinks by his teammates in the clubhouse locker room—razors, shave cream, soap, deodorant—Yogi would simply help himself to whatever he needed. Players were becoming increasingly annoyed by this bothersome habit until one player finally decided to fix Yogi's wagon. He deliberately left a roll-on deodorant on the sink with its top removed. The devious player then applied crazy glue to the roll-on ball of the antiperspirant.

Later, when the game ended at Yankee Stadium that afternoon, the players showered, dressed, and left the building. Suddenly, those outside in the parking lot heard an ear-splitting scream emanating from the clubhouse. It was Yogi. His arms were stuck to his sides!

On August 17th, 1957, in Philadelphia, the most bizarre incident occurred during a game against the Giants. Hall-of-Famer Richie Ashburn hit a foul ball that struck Alice Roth, seated in a box seat next to her two grandsons. The ball hit her squarely in the face, breaking her nose. As the medics were carrying Mrs. Roth away on a stretcher, Ashburn fouled off the very next pitch thrown to him. The ball struck Roth again, this time breaking a bone in her knee! She was the wife of the Sports Editor for the *Philadelphia Bulletin*.

Everything ended happily, with the kids treated royally and Ashburn visiting Alice the next day in the hospital. They became good friends. The odds of a fan being hit just once by a foul ball are 300,000 to 1.

Finally, at the turn of the century, there was a "singing umpire," Bill "Lord" Byron. He would serenade a batter who took a called third strike with the lyrics, *"Let me tell you something son, before you get much older… you cannot hit the ball, my friend, with the bat upon your shoulder!"*

Can you imagine Byron serenading Ty Cobb?

January 31, 2021

Sources: Baseball: A History of America's Favorite Game-George Vecsey; Baseball: AnIllustrated History-Geoffrey C. Ward and Ken Burns; Google-Baseball Idioms for Everyday English; Wikipedia, The Seven Year Itch.

GIANTS, DODGERS AND A BRAWL FOR THE AGES

"Baseball fights can be more dangerous than hockey fights, where two players square off, because you've got guys running all over the place and people throwing punches at you that you don't see half the time."— Tom Glavine

The Giants/Dodgers storied rivalry officially started in 1890 when Brooklyn joined the National League. The Giants occupied the Polo grounds in the so called "classier" borough of Manhattan, while the Dodgers held forth in the blue collar borough of Brooklyn. As the calendar continued its assent into the final decade of the 19th century, the rivalry began heating up as if jabbed by a red-hot poker.

The long standing personal feud between Brooklyn owner, Charles Ebbets, and Giants manager, John "Muggsy" McGraw, intensified and a palpable hatred began to develop between the two teams. In 1940, Bill Terry knew the Dodgers were "still in the league" and their followers could be ferocious. Umpire George Magerkurth was brutally beaten by an enraged Dodger fan ostensibly for making a pro Giants call. Around the same time, my dad was seated in the upper deck in left field, at Ebbets Field. He was standing, cheering the Giants. As he settled back into his seat, he felt a harsh tap on his shoulder. My father turned and looked into the angry eyes of a guy with arms like tree trunks. The Brooklyn fan forcefully asked, "Was you rootin' for the Giants, Buddy?" From that point on my dad made a concerted effort to curb his enthusiasm for the visiting team.

Starting in 1951, many of the pennant races between the two clubs were legendary. We all know about *The Shot Heard 'Round the World,* made possible by the Giants winning 37 of 44 games to catch the Dodgers and force a three game playoff.

!959 was also a doozy. The San Fran Giants led the LA Dodgers by three games as late as September 6—only to be swept two weeks later by the same Dodgers and eliminated. This enabled LA to catch the Milwaukee Braves and beat them the first two games of a three game playoff, then vanquish the Go-Go White Sox in six games. This was mainly due to the "cannon for an arm" possessed by Dodger catcher John Roseboro, curtailing the White Sox great base stealing speed. John also contributed the winning hit in game three. (We'll spare Dodgers fans 1962)

At the 1965 Academy Awards, My Fair Lady won eight Oscars and on March 25, Martin Luther King, Jr. concluded a four day march from Selma to Montgomery, Alabama, along with 25,000 civil rights proponents. Also, the Giants and Dodgers put on another remarkable pennant race.

The Giants won 14 straight and 17 of 18 games approaching the last two weeks of September, poised on the top step of victory--when they

SOME CATCH!

exhaled. The Dodgers then concluded a 13 in a row streak and 15 of 16 to advance to the WS! LA beat the Minnesota Twins in a seven game thriller. But along the way, a shocking event took place on August 22, at Candlestick Park, San Francisco.

The Dodgers were a game and a half ahead of the Giants, as two HOF pitchers opposed each other: Sandy Koufax and Juan Marichal.

Maury Wills led off with a bunt single and scored the first run on a Ron Fairly double. Marichal thought bunting was a cheap way to get on and when Wills faced him again Juan knocked him down. This called for retaliation when Willie Mays stepped into the batter's box. Now, Koo Foo was a complete, soft spoke gentleman who just couldn't throw at a batter. But he sounded more like Leo Durocher when the pitching maestro once said, "Show me a guy who can't pitch inside and I'll show you a loser." So, did he dust Willie? Not on your life. He aimed the next pitch a mile over Mays' head!

The next inning Marichal sent Ron Fairly sprawling with nasty chin music. Tempers flared. Roseboro told teammates, "I'll take care of it." When Marichal came to bat Roseboro, on the third pitch, deliberately whistled the return throw to Koufax, possibly clipping the tip of Marichal's ear. As John rose from his crouch, Juan swung his bat and hit the side of Roseboro's head at least twice. Blood poured out. The infuriated backstop immediately tried to attack the rival pitcher. (Marichal claimed the next day, "I thought he was going to hit me with his mask so I hit him with my bat.")

At the sight of their bleeding catcher, enraged Dodgers charged towards the plate. Left fielder Lou Johnson, wild with anger, was suddenly hoisted up in a bear hug by behemoth Willie McCovey, who gently placed him out of harm's way. Meanwhile, Giants captain Willie Mays, tears in his eyes, pulled his close friend back and guided him into the Dodger's dugout with a towel pressed to his bloody skull. That seemed to end the brawl. Johnson proclaimed, "Willie Mays was the hero, his action stopped what could have been much worse."

Marichal was suspended for eight days (10 games) and fined a mere $1750. Both pitchers struggled a bit in their next few starts.

Dodgers GM Buzzy Bavasi said Roseboro "was the best .240 hitter in baseball history." John was also an intelligent field general and considered the premier defensive catcher in the 1960's. Loved by his pitchers, Roseboro caught two of the four Sandy Koufax no-hitters. Very quiet and spoke in a whisper, thus his nickname, "Gabby."

Roseboro finally buried the hatchet with Marichal and when Juan was ironically signed by the Dodgers in 1975, they had become good friends. John campaigned for Marichal's induction into the Hall in 1983, realizing the delay was because of the "incident." No one could argue with the Dominican Dandy's glittering stats, which included 243 victories, three years with 25 plus wins, and a 16 year career 2.89 ERA. He's still robust at 85, living in Santo Domingo and currently serving as the Minister of Sports for the Dominican government.

Roseboro had some difficult times in baseball toward the end of his 14 year career, but did appear in TV commercials, as well as a few films afterward. He succumbed to heart disease in 2002. Marichal served as an honorary pall bearer at the funeral.

He said poignantly, "Johnny's forgiving me was one of the best things that happened in my life. I wish I could have had John Roseboro as my catcher."

November 22, 2022

Sources: Wikipedia; SABR article by Warren Corbett; schedule almanac Dodgers/Giants, '65; Baseball America on line; Baseball ref: Roseboro, Marichal

THE NEW YORK METS' FAMOUS "SIGN MAN"

Karl Kurt Ehrhardt was born in Unterweissbach, Germany, on November 26, 1924, the son of Willie and Elsie Voight Ehrhardt. When he was six the family arrived in the United States, and Karl spent his boyhood growing up in the Ridgewood section of Brooklyn and attending Grover Cleveland High School.

As part of his Army tour during WWII, he spent three years in Europe and served as a translator in a prisoner-of-war camp holding German soldiers. He returned home to marry, raise a family and pursue a career as Art Director in the sales promotion department for American Home Foods. But the great adventure that made Karl Ehrhardt famous began at Shea Stadium in 1965.

When the Dodgers and Giants left town after the 1957 season, fans felt abandoned and bitter about their move to the West Coast. As a loyal Brooklyn rooter, there was a baseball void in his life until the New York Mets moved into the Polo Grounds at 155th St. in Harlem, in 1962. It was nice to have a National League team in the City again, but Karl didn't start going to the games until Shea Stadium opened its doors the year of the New York World's Fair, in 1964.

Karl would sit way up on top, in the far reaches of the upper deck. Henny Youngman, king of the one-liners, would've had a field day. "Ehrhardt was up so high he was getting spirit messages. He got halfway up, and the usher stopped. Ehrhardt said, 'What's the matter with you?' The usher replied, 'I don't go any farther, after this my nose starts to bleed.'" You get the picture. But it was baseball and Karl was where he was supposed to be.

One summer day in 1965, Karl decided to make use of his creative talent. He constructed a huge 30 ft. sign and hung it from the mezzanine facade behind third base. With a white and black format, the sign was visible all over the ballpark. Referring to both the stodgy M. Donald Grant, the Mets' Chairman of the Board, and the general state of the team at the time, the sign read, WELCOME TO GRANT'S TOMB. As Karl at the time recalled:

"Suddenly, during the National Anthem, six maintenance guys came running down the aisle, tore the sign down and ran back up the aisle. I just sat there like a dummy, not knowing how to react. I decided to go down to the press level. I was able to tell Steve Jacobson, a young reporter with Newsday at the time, what happened. He wrote about it in his column the next day, bemoaning 'Censorship at Shea.' I found out it was actually a security man named Matt Burns who ordered the sign taken down."

A few days later, Karl went back with another sign, which read, WE SCRIBBLE, WHILE MATT BURNS. More ink in the local papers and... *The Sign Man* was born!

The next year, 1966, Karl's typographer (an expert in the appearance of printed matter) for American Home Foods, got two season box tickets, section 72E about 20 feet up, directly behind the visiting teams' dugout. The tickets were for Tuesday and Friday night games during every Mets homestand. For the next 14 years, 1966-1979, Karl occupied one of those seats entertaining the fans with his signs. The final year and a half of the Sign Man's run, 1980 through the strike-shortened 1981 season, were courtesy of the Mets' Fred Wilpon. He provided Karl with his own special box seat and free parking, along with a place to change into his familiar garb for the game.

My memory of The Sign Man is strong. His beaming smile, as he would spring from his seat with just the right sign at the right time. The black derby hat with the yellow shirt (after the '73 World Series, the shirt became blue because yellow was too close to the Oakland A's colors); the signs held high and rotated perfectly for the crowd and TV cameras. I loved "LOOK MA, NO HANDS," when an infielder booted a ground ball. "I was always half a ham," Karl said in our phone conversation, "I really got into it. The derby was the gimmick I needed as things evolved. It was a lot of work but truly a labor of love."

Talk about work. Each sign was really two signs, because the fans demanded both sides of the panel contain the message, so nobody would miss one of Karl's gems. The signs were made of black buckeye (cardboard stock) using 20x26 panels. He spent hours preparing about 60 signs per game geared toward a specific match-up, and a gut feeling about whether the game would be a slugfest or a low scoring affair. As a play or situation developed, Karl would have two or three signs ready for that event. When it happened he then jumped up with the color-coded sign that best matched the words with the action. He would do this maybe a dozen times a game. "The logistics began to be overwhelming. At the end, I had over 1300 signs and to select 50 or 60 for a game was quite a task."

I asked Karl if there were ever an adverse reaction by a player to a sign he flashed:

> "Yes, in the beginning, Bill. I was never enamored of the talents of Ed Kranepool. So, I couldn't resist. I came up with the sign, *SUPER STIFF*...he gave me a withering look, even

though the crowd was tickled. We had words at a couple of Old Timers luncheons. I finally said, 'Ed, it's all in good fun.' He bellowed back, 'Yeah, at my expense!' But after that, it was better. And we actually got to be pretty good friends. He was a good guy."

In 1973, the Mets invited Karl and his wife, Lucille, to join the club in Oakland for the finale of the 1973 World Series. He borrowed $200 from his mom for the flight and they were on their way.

The trip led to one of Karl's most memorable signs. Charles O. Finley, the screwball owner of the A's, had recently dismissed the Oakland starting second baseman, Mike Andrews, because of an unfortunate error early in the Series. The uncalled-for move by the power-crazed owner had made all the papers and the man with the signs was just waiting for his opportunity:

> "Luckily, the A's third baseman, Sal Bando, made an error in one of the early innings. I couldn't wait to jump up. I was ready with, *YOU'RE FIRED!* Finley was only a couple of rows away, he looked daggers at me!!"

As Ehrhardt's fame gained momentum, he was a guest on several TV shows, including Mike Douglas and To Tell the Truth. But Karl was most proud of his innovative signs. Ralph Kiner's favorite was, *JOSE, CAN YOU SEE?* That one was hoisted up when Jose Cardinal struck out. During the 1969 World Series, Karl made the papers with, *THE ORIOLES ARE FOR THE BIRDS!* More than one dirty look flashed from the Baltimore dugout. But The Sign Man saved his masterpiece for Game Five of that World Series.

The grand moment arrived. Davey Johnson lofted a long fly ball to deep left field. Cleon Jones corralled it about a foot in front of the warning track, dropping to one knee as he squeezed the baseball for the final out. The Mets were world champions in only the eighth year of their existence! Karl's four-word sign will never be forgotten:

THERE ARE NO WORDS

Those were the perfect words. His last signs pierced the Shea Stadium air in the summer of 1981. For several years, he continued to do birthday party signs for local business clubs. As he recalled for me:

> "It got to be an enormous amount of work. Plus, the team was losing and I was emotionally involved. I just felt it was time to call it a day. Although, I did feel lost, like a withdrawal period, for about two years afterward."

One of my jobs for an area business was to write baseball stories for the company magazine. I called Jay Horwitz, Mets Media VP, and he gave me Karl's contact info. Jay was very pleasant. Karl was just as nice, and we had several fun phone conversations, in 2000.

The Sign Man passed away February 5, 2008 at his home in Glen Oaks, Queens. He was 83. No image will ever be more vivid than that of the effervescent Ehrhardt, popping up with his sign, with just the right phrase to capture a baseball moment.

December 12, 2020

Sources: interviews w/K. Ehrhardt; Wikipedia, Karl Ehrhardt; NY Times, Sign Man obituary; Henny Youngman one-liner comedy.

TOM SEAVER INTERVIEW, PRELUDE TO A MIRACLE... AND MORE

It was Monday afternoon, April 14 1969, during the penultimate year of Connie Mack Stadium's existence. The Mets would lose to the Philadelphia Phillies 5-1. It was the fourth game in a four-game losing streak for the Amazins. By late afternoon they would be 2-5 on the season. It was the same old "you know what" for a losing team.

But about an hour before the first pitch, News Director Phil Hubbard and I had flashed our press passes signifying we were from WOBM-FM in Toms River, NJ. The usher waved us right onto the field, past the field boxes, about halfway between home plate and third base. We were hot stuff, man! Not realizing luck was on our side, and that perhaps it would not be so easy another time. With our tape recorder all set to go, we spotted Tom Seaver doing wind sprints about 50 feet away down the left-field line.

Baseball's first steel-and-concrete stadium loomed in the background, now a hideous anachronism, with a handful of fans rattling around in the sprawling, rickety lower grandstand. We got a little closer and I shouted, "Hey, Tom, could you spare a minute for a quick interview?" He immediately stopped in mid-sprint and came right over. I was too stunned to be nervous. He was super nice - treated me like I was Vin Scully. I blurted out a few banalities and then asked the Mets' best pitcher, "Do you think the Mets, with a few breaks, might have the nucleus to be contenders this year?" (I didn't believe a word of it, the Mets were coming off their best season since their inception in 1962. But they finished 73-89, still 16 games below the breakeven mark). Seaver responded enthusiastically, "Bill, as you say, with a few breaks I really think we have the talent to contend this year." He pointed out pitching would be the key. I thanked him profusely. And the soon to be National League Cy Young winner went back to his wind sprints. Little did we know…

In 1969, they lowered the pitcher's mound and the fortunes of the New York Metropolitans soared. It was the first season of the divisional format. For the first 41 games, they looked a tad better than for most of their brief history but were only 18-23 at the start of games on May 28. Then, Tom Seaver's words about pitching resonated in a big way. In perhaps the best outing of his career, Jerry Koosman dominated the San Diego Padres for 10 innings, yielding no runs on just four hits and striking out 15 Padre batters! The Mets won 1-0 in 11 innings, with Buddy Harrelson driving in the winning run and Tug McGraw getting the W in relief. The victory started an 11 game winning streak and fans knew this was a different team.

A catalytic force in the Mets climb was the acquisition of Donn Clendenon on June 15, in a trade with the Montreal Expos, for pitcher Steve Renko, Kevin Collins, two minor leaguers and a player to be named later. Clendenon was a solid slugger for the Expos but in need of a change of scenery. Manager Gil Hodges platooned the righty power hitter with Ed Kranepool at first base in what proved a brilliant move. In just 202 at-bats, Clendenon clubbed 12 home runs with 37 RBI. Donn would be the World Series MVP with three homers and a .357 batting average.

But the Chicago Cubs got out of the gate 11-1. And before you could blink, they were 41-19 on June 15. On the same day, the Mets were 30-26. On June 30, the Sports Illustrated cover had a picture of rugged Ron Santo leading off first base with the headline, *The Raucous New Cubs*. Chicago had a nice team: Williams, Santo and Banks would account for 73 HR and 324 RBI. Beckert and Kessinger were a first-class double play combo. And the pitching was solid: Jenkins, Hands and Holtzman combined for 58 wins and Dick Selma could throw 100 mph. Phil Regan anchored the bullpen. The little bears were lapping up every minute of it, as was their fiery manager Leo Durocher. Santo would click his heels after every Wrigley Field win. This antic infuriated some but, what the heck - it was a harmless home crowd pleaser.

The night of July 9 saw the Mets tie the season's series with the Cubs at five games apiece, winning 4-0. However, the real story was Tom Seaver's near-perfect game. With one out in the top of the ninth, Jimmy Qualls lined a Tom Terrific off-speed pitch to left-center for a clean hit to spoil the perfect game and no-hitter. Nearly 60,000 at Shea were crushed when the ball fell safely. But they would have much to cheer about before the historic season ended.

It was a mesmerizing Mets baseball season. In January, it was said some casinos were offering 1000-to-1 odds against the Amazins winning the Fall Classic. But quietly a team under the auspices of lovable Gil Hodges was beginning to coalesce. Tommy Agee (26 HR) and Cleon Jones (.340 BA) were having career years. Donn Clendenon was rejuvenated. And a starting rotation of Seaver (25-7, 2.21 ERA), Koosman (17-9, 2.28 ERA), Nolan Ryan and Gary Gentry, with Tug McGraw and Ron Taylor in the bullpen, comprised a formidable nucleus. Not to mention the remarkable Ron Swoboda, Art Shamsky, Grote, Garrett, Ed Charles, Al Weiss et al.

So, what happened? The Cubs held a nine-game lead over the Cardinals and Mets on August 17, with a 75-44 record. Then, in September,

Chicago wilted under the pressure of the Mets' relentless winning. They lost 11 of 12, September 3-15, going from 5 games up to 4 ½ games behind New York. From Sept. 6-18, the Mets went 13-1. The Cubs, playing games on the west coast, could see the Mets' winning final score before they even started play.

On September 9 the Cubs lost the famous "Black Cat" game, in which a black cat walked past Ron Santo, in the on-deck circle at Shea Stadium, and allegedly stopped and stared at Leo Durocher.

Nolan Ryan tossed a three-hitter in the second game of a doubleheader, on September 10, leading the Mets to a victory over the expos and moving them into first place in the National East for the first time in franchise history.

The Cubs said Durocher was intractable and refused to rest anyone. He barely used Dick Selma down the stretch and pitched his top three starters until their arms hung like strings. Leo's take was a little different, "I never saw anything like it in my life. Our offense went down the toilet. The defense went down the drain. And I'm still looking for the pitching staff. I could have dressed nine broads up as ballplayers and they would have beaten the Cubs."

Ron Swoboda said this about his team, "We had the innocence of someone who had never been there before. We had that wonderful, clear-minded innocence…of not having to doubt ourselves if we stumbled. That's a marvelous thing…the Cubs just found they were in a race with a faster horse."

Ron Santo said,

> "What's hard for me to believe is how we were eight games in front and lost by eight games. That just goes to show you that it was the year of the Mets and that God lives in New York."

Santo knew something. How else would you explain the Mets beating Steve Carlton and the Cards 4-3 on Sept. 15, with two 2-run home runs by Ron Swoboda, when Carlton set a major league record with 19 strikeouts? Or, winning both games of a twin bill on September 12, at Pittsburgh, by the identical scores of 1-0, with the winning pitchers Koosman and Cardwell knocking in the lone runs in each game?

The magic continued through the postseason. As Mickey Mantle exclaimed, "I never did see catches like that in a World Series!" Two gems by Tommie Agee that saved multiple runs and the greatest catch ever in a World Series by Ron Swoboda. His impossible grab, robbing Brooks Robinson in Game Four, kept the miracle alive and made sure the mighty Orioles would not likely take the Series back to Baltimore.

The 1969 Mets were the personification of team play. And Gil Hodges was the perfect manager for that group, never allowing his players to "put pressure above the pleasure of playing the game."

At the end of this COVID 19 short form baseball season, we just might hear Peter Alonso, with champaign soaked hair, paraphrase Tom Seaver in the Mets locker room, 51 years ago, "We're just a bunch of young kids who love to play this game!"

July 29, 2020

Sources: Shibe Park, Connie Mack Stadium: History Sports Illustrated-1969 archives; The Cubs' collapse of 1969: An oral history-Chicago Tribune; 1969 Mets schedule almanac; 1969 Cubs schedule almanac; 1969 Mets, Cubs rosters and stats.

THE AMAZING STORY OF REX BARNEY

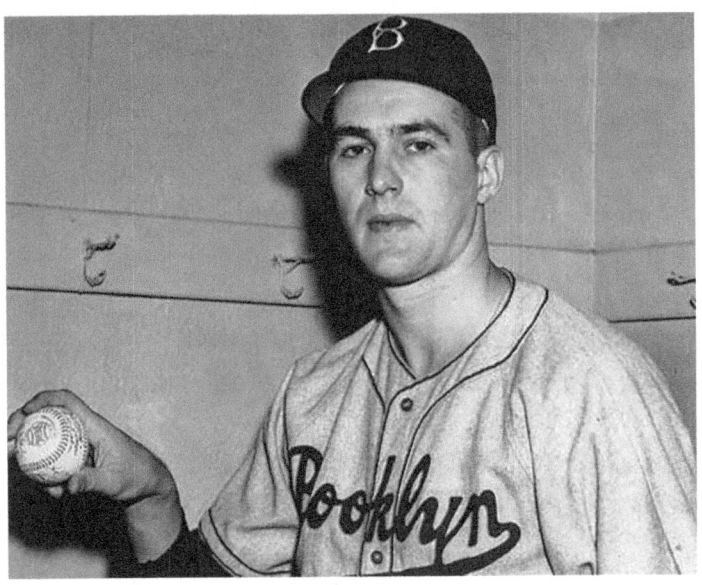

"I should have been up there with the greats. I should have gone right up the ladder, but too many rungs were missing." -Rex Barney

Pitcher's elbow, also known as medial epicondyle apophysate, is a common injury that occurs among young baseball players. It can be caused by overuse and repetitive motion. Pain and swelling explode inside the elbow. Range of motion and even the ability to throw a ball is often diminished. Plain and simple, pitching is an unnatural movement that puts unnatural stress on the elbow and shoulder joints. When I was an 11-year-old pitching against older kids, I had some success throwing a curveball. But snapping my wrist upon releasing the ball would twist my arm into a pretzel of pain for days! So throwing too hard and spinning the breaking ball at a tender age may eventually account for many disabling pitching injuries later on at the professional level. But what accounts for a successful major league pitcher losing control and never regaining his command? This is the story of one such pitcher who plunged into the abyss of terminal wildness.

Born in an elevator on the way up to the delivery room on December 19, 1924, Rex Edward Barney came into the world on a 20 degree below zero night in Omaha Nebraska. Rex was the youngest of four children of Marie and Edward Spencer Barney. He was a star basketball and baseball player at Creighton Prep, a Catholic school for boys in Omaha. Basketball was his best sport.

Eighteen-year-old Rex Barney signed with the Brooklyn Dodgers for a $2500 bonus in 1943. In his first start against the Chicago Cubs, he promptly plunked lead-off batter Eddie Stanky squarely in the middle of the back, serving as an unfortunate omen of things to come. Yes, the hard-throwing 6' 3" 185-pounder was just a wee bit wild. But that was not unusual for one so young. Barney enlisted in the Army in September of that year. Two years later, he found himself the commander of a lead tank in the 6th Armored Division in Germany. He suffered shrapnel wounds and won two Purple Hearts and a Bronze Star. Back with Brooklyn in 1946, Rex was regarded as a serious fireballer but "pitched as though the plate was high and outside."

Two mediocre seasons morphed into 1948, when he won 15 games and posted a nifty 3.10 ERA. He fanned 138 in 246 innings, and for the only time in his career, struck out more batters than he walked. The lean right-hander pitched a one-hitter against the Cubs in August with the only hit a dying quail off the bat of Ralph "Putsy" Caballero in the seventh inning. Barney then dominated the Giants at the Polo grounds with a dazzling no-hitter on a damp Thursday night, September 9. He even had to endure a one-hour rain delay. Home plate umpire Babe Pinelli was impressed:

"He's the fastest thing in baseball today. I don't care about Lemon or Feller. I've seen them. This kid is it. And no finer boy in baseball could have pitched it. He has a heart as big as a lion and a wonderful disposition."

SOME CATCH!

My dad and I, inveterate Giants fans, also thought Rex Barney had arrived. He was one of those exciting pitchers always capable of notching a no-hitter. However, Barney regressed the next year, and in 1950, he was walking nearly 13 batters per nine innings with a bloated 6.42 ERA. That was his final campaign in the major leagues.

The Dodgers optioned Rex to Fort Worth of the Texas League in 1951. In a game against Houston, Barney broke the league record for walks issued by a pitcher in a game. He surrendered 16 free passes in seven and two-third innings. In 1952, his pitching line for the American Association St. Paul Saints read: four games, three innings pitched, no wins, one loss, 14 walks, and 17 earned runs, with a catastrophic 51.00 ERA! Sadly, Rex Barney's professional baseball career was over.

The 28-year-old Barney was despondent. He even thought of pulling the plug on his life. But then he remembered the words of legendary broadcaster Red Barber a decade earlier, "Son, you have a pleasing radio voice. You should consider broadcasting beyond your pitching career." And so he did. From a 250-watt station in Vero Beach, Florida, Barney found his way to the Game-of-the-Day on Mutual Radio. He was then hired by WOR-TV to work with Al Helfer in1958, broadcasting National League games to New York. I remember hearing the name "Rex Barney" and was surprised to be listening to such a pro on the air!

Life, like a baseball, takes funny bounces. The next broadcasting adventure for the former Dodger came with the help of Lee MacPhail, the Baltimore Orioles' general manager. Lee had been an office boy during Rex's early Brooklyn Dodger days. Barney began a gig as a sports talk show host in Baltimore in 1965 and became a celebrity in his new favorite city.

In the late '60s, the ex-hurler began filling in for Bill Bolling, the public address announcer at Memorial Stadium. In the spring of '73, he became the Orioles' regular PA man, a job he held during the move to Camden Yards and until he passed away in August, 1997. His famous cry, "Give that fan a contract!" after a patron made a nice snag of a ball in the stands, became part of the Baltimore culture. "His voice was like a security blanket" said TV announcer and former Oriole 20-game winner, Mike Flannagan.

But why, after a fine, coming-into-his-own season in 1948, did Rex Barney begin to seriously wobble and finally lose all semblance of control? Barney and others believed that a broken ankle, suffered sliding into second base on the final day of the 1948 season, forced him to alter his pitching style:

"In 1949 I won nine ballgames but from then on I never had the same motion, never had it again. I never got into the same flow, and in baseball everything is rhythm."

The fates allowed Rex to pitch in a Dodger uniform for only a short time. But he savored every minute he wore number 26. In the words of the amiable Nebraskan, "The Brooklyn Dodgers, Ebbets Field, and baseball was the greatest triple play God ever executed on this planet."

February 21, 2021

Sources: Rex Barney page, Wikipedia; Society for American Baseball Research (SABR) article on Rex Barney, by Don Harrison; Rex Barney page of Baseball-Reference.com; Brooklyn Dodger 1948 schedule almanac; Pitcher's elbow information: Excerpts edited from Wikipedia.

RANDOM MUSINGS OF A LIFE-LONG GIANTS FAN

BASEBALL UNPLUGGED

Here we go again, nudging the floodgates open just a tad to allow a modest stream of intriguing baseball humor, history, and wisdom - from our vast archives.

Paraphrasing 1950s TV news anchor and later Timex pitchman, John Cameron Swayze, we'll hopscotch the decades for anecdotes to rivet your attention. One or two on a personal note, others researched with meticulous care.

MY FIRST GAME

Many things are remembered vividly from the age of six, but there are gaps. This is what sticks with me from that long-ago day, like it was yesterday. From Westfield, New Jersey my dad and I took the 222 bus to the Port Authority Bus Terminal in Manhattan (41st and 8th). After a short subway ride to 59th at Columbus Circle, we hopped on the express "D" train. It seemed to roar at breakneck speed immediately, with a rushing, hypnotic clackety-clack din as the stations flew by in a blur--20 minutes, two stops, and then...155th St. and 8th Avenue. Coogan's Bluff-the Polo Grounds!

The first sight of the famous ballpark was breathtaking; the infield dirt seemed flawless; lush, green grass way out into the open spaces of the huge outfield. And double decks extending around the bullpens at the curve of the horseshoe stadium in left and right center, meeting the two bleacher sections in center field divided by a recessed clubhouse—505 feet from home plate at that time, in 1944.

It was a June 11th Sunday doubleheader with the Phillies. I was enthralled with the whole thing but remember only one specific event, occurring in the first game. We were halfway back in the lower deck equidistant between home plate and third base. A left-handed batter was up for the Giants around the fifth inning (Johnny Rucker maybe). He hit a drive on one hop to the Phils' right fielder. The cheering crowd was on its feet, including my dad. But in my child's mind, if the ball didn't go over the fence it wasn't so great. I said, "Aw, that's no good." My father snapped, "It's a hit you damn fool, it's a hit!" I shut up. The Giants won both games. On the way home I asked if they ever played a triple header. My baseball mentor knew he had a burgeoning fanatic on his hands.

OH, THOSE EARLY DAYS

Before the turn of the 20th century, only one umpire would work a regular major league baseball game. This allowed baserunners to take extraordinary liberties when they knew the man in blue was looking elsewhere. "Run with one eye on the ball and the other on the umpire." For example, if the ump were occupied with action at second base, a baserunner coming around third would cut 15 feet off his path and not bother touching the base at all.

In Cincinnati, circa 1898, National League Hall-of-Fame first baseman, Jake Beckley took outrageous advantage and came around to score without a play being made on him. Umpire Tim Hurst, whose attention had been diverted, nonetheless called Beckley out at the plate. "You got here too quick," Hurst told the first sacker.

TY COBB

With his .366 lifetime batting average, 12 batting titles, and dominant base stealing exploits, the Georgia Peach is still considered by many the greatest player of all time. But It was widely agreed Ty Cobb had a severe persecution complex, which made him a horrifying figure both on and off the field. Even Cobb himself, in later years characterized his youthful self as "a snarling wildcat." Teammate Davey Jones said, "He had such a rotten disposition that it was almost impossible to be his friend."

In his autobiography, Ty acknowledged that during the 1909 season he decided to scare off Boston pitcher Cy Morgan, who Cobb insisted had been throwing at his head. Positioned at second base, Tyrus Raymond got his chance when Morgan uncorked a wild pitch. Cobb was determined to race all the way home, anticipating a violent collision with his nemesis, as the pitcher covered the plate. Cobb had barely rounded third when Morgan was ready at home plate, waiting with the ball. "As I came down the line and went whipping at him with my steel showing," Cobb wrote, "Morgan…turned and actually ran away from the plate. I scored, and Morgan was released by Boston that night."

THE WINNING STREAK CONTINUES…WITH A TWIST

It was a glorious, euphoric time for Giants fans as Sunday, August 26, 1951, blossomed into a perfect late summer day. The team had won 12 straight games and my dad and I couldn't wait to get to the Polo

Grounds and watch the twin bill with the Cubs, as our beloveds would surely extend to 14 in a row. Sal Maglie had great stuff in that first game, fanning eight little bears over eight innings with the Giants breezing 4-1.

Meanwhile, over at Ebbets Field, "dem bums" were blasting the Pirates 9-3 in the top of the seventh, in their first of two. Then fans with radios started cheering in scattered pockets throughout the stands. Suddenly a huge "8" went up on the scoreboard for the Bucs. They would go on to beat Brooklyn 12-11. It just didn't get any better!

But a funny thing happened in the Chicago ninth inning. Maglie had thrown a ton of pitches and was tired. With two on and one out the Cubs sent in a very tall, angular left-handed pinch hitter. He was thin with a face carved out of granite. The game was wrapped up—but suddenly it wasn't. This huge character, a cross between Ichabod Crane and James Arness, swatted a long drive deep into the lower deck in right field to tie the game. How dare he do that! And the blow knocked Sal out of the game, relieved by Sheldon "Available" Jones. The Giants prevailed 5-4 in the bottom of the ninth. But who was this towering batter who knocked our best pitcher out of the game?

He was one of only 13 athletes to play both professional basketball (Boston Celtics, '47) and major league baseball (Dodgers,'50; Cubs '51). He pursued a freelance acting career on TV and in 1958 was the star of The Rifleman, which was enormously popular and ran for five years. Got it? Yup, it was Chuck Connors. How about that?

A COGENT QUOTE

It's a wild time in baseball, where pitchers are so profoundly dominant, throwing fastballs that make the radar gun wince at 102 mph. And pitches that whoosh through the hitting zone, while diving a half foot at the knees.

Cincinnati slugger Ted Kluszewski, years ago, offered this analogy concerning the difficulty of connecting with a major league pitched ball that seems particularly appropriate today:

"How hard is hitting?" asked Big Klu, rhetorically. "You ever walk into a pitch-black room full of furniture that you've never seen before and try to walk through it without bumping into anything? Well, it's harder than that."

That's all for now, folks. But stay tuned, we're just getting started!

June 2, 2021

STAN MUSIAL: THE BEGINNING-THE CRISIS- THE THIRD MVP

How good was Stan Musial? He was good enough to take your breath away - Vin Scully

He could hit .300 with a fountain pen -Joe Garagiola

"Whaddya say, whaddya say!" was Stan Musial's standard, smiling greeting. When he reported to Al Lang Field in St. Petersburg, Florida to begin spring training in late February 1947, things looked awfully good. The St. Louis Cardinals were World Series champions for the third time in five years and Stan, just back from a year in the Navy, had won the National League batting title for the second time in three years, posting a lofty .365 average. He was also coming off his second MVP season and, at 26, was a superstar by all measures. Though Musial looked slightly thin and wan as he prepared for the upcoming season, no one was concerned at the time. The war was over and folks had other diversions:

A supposed extraterrestrial spacecraft was reported near Roswell, New Mexico.

"The Best Years of Our Lives" won the Academy Award for Best Picture of 1946.

And after two weeks in the welcoming Florida sun, Musial was now nicely bronzed and looked much better. The classic coiled crouch deep in the batter's box was intact but the ringing line drives were few and far between. But this wasn't the first spring he'd started slowly. Another banner year for number 6, batting third in the Cardinal lineup, was predicted.

Flash Back

The life of the Hall of Fame player began 27 years earlier, courtesy of Lukasz and Mary Lancos Musial in Donora, Pennsylvania. The fifth of six children, Stanislaw Franciszek Musial was born on November 21, 1920 to a Polish immigrant father and a mother of Carpatho-Rusyn decent. When he enrolled in school, his name was anglicized to Stanley frank Musial.

Stan was known at Donora high school for his ready smile and profound ability to play baseball and basketball. His dad, Lukasz, fully expected him to be working in the local steel mill or zinc works by the time he was 18. Actually, Stan was the only one of the six Musial children to graduate Donora with a high school diploma. But before he graduated, he was also a professional ballplayer-having signed a contract with the St. Louis Cardinals' Monessen club of the class D Penn State League two months before his 17th birthday. He was playing baseball for the high school, then for the pros in the summer.

(And "The Donora Greyhound" could fly. Over the span of nine years, '46-'54, he led the National League in runs scored five times, averaging 119 per year).

In 1940, he married his high school sweetheart-pretty, petite Lillian Labash (72 year marriage, 4 children). He also met his greatest friend and mentor, Dickie Kerr, who managed the Daytona Beach Islanders in the Class D Florida State League. Kerr had two complete game victories for the Chicago White Sox in the 1919 World Series against the Cincinnati Reds (including a shutout, and a 1.42 ERA). He won his games while most of his teammates were tanking for gamblers who bet on the opposition.

Like Kerr, Stan was a left handed pitcher and, under his manager's tutelage, was pitching well and playing the outfield between starts to take advantage of his awesome hitting prowess. Then disaster struck in centerfield. Musial dove for a liner and fell heavily on his left shoulder. The pain was excruciating and Stan feared this could be the end of his pitching career. After a couple of bad outings, the kid told Kerr he might as well go back home and work in the steel mills. "No Stan, don't give up like that," Dickie advised quickly. "This is a great game and you can still make it. As a pitcher, no. But the way you can hit, the managers in the upper leagues wouldn't fool around with you as a pitcher anyway. They'd want you in there every day, instead of every fourth game. Stay with it, kid, this is a great game. You won't be happy out of it."

Good advice. Branch Rickey ordered he be moved up to Class C in Springfield Missouri. Musial strengthened his weakened throwing arm and pounded the baseball. Before you could blink Stan was up with the big club in St. Louis, in September of 1941, and stayed for 22 years.

The Turning Point

As the season opened in 1947, The Donora Greyhound was still not hitting and batted .146 in April. Into May, nothing changed. One newspaper even had teammate Enos Slaughter giving Musial a savage beating, in a fist fight. Musial, outraged by the rumor, piped up, "Country and I have been good friends for years. Nothing could be further from the truth!" Then, in his typical kindly manner, Stan allowed, "Well, I guess his publisher put pressure on him to get a story. I bear him no grudge."

A crisis seemed imminent when he took to his hotel bed with a throbbing pain in his lower right abdomen. The diagnosis was acute appendicitis. One doctor advised against moving Musial at all, for fear the appendix would burst. An operation was necessary, immediately. But Stan insisted he first see the club surgeon, Dr. Robert F. Hyland in St. Louis. Hyland shocked everyone by announcing Musial would miss only a few games—he would freeze the appendix by judiciously placing ice packs around the organ. This treatment produced dramatic results in similar cases, and it worked for Stan. Five days after the May 9th procedure, "The Man" was back in the lineup and quickly regained form. From June through September he hit .342 and raised his average to a fine .312, with 95 runs batted in for the season. But Musial referred to it as "that lousy year." After the season, Stan had his appendix removed along with his tonsils.

1948 saw "Stan The Man" put up numbers seldom equaled in baseball history. Stan was batting .415 heading into the second week of July and ultimately led the NL with a .376 average (only because he "slumped" to .348 in August to diminish his final number!). He topped the senior circuit with 131 RBI, 50 doubles, 20 triples and an OPS+ of 200. He batted .416 against left handed pitching.

He missed the Triple Crown by a single homer, smashing 39 to trail Ralph Kiner and Johnny Mize—each belting 40 to lead the Majors. There have been reports that Musial lost a home run in a rainout and another where he was credited with a ground rule double when a blast at Sportsman's Park should have been ruled a homerun. But no box score or definitive record of either event occurring that year could be found. He won his third and final MVP award.

One of the most amiable men to ever walk the planet, Stan may have left baseball with more friends than anyone in the history of the game.

March 9, 2021

Sources: Stan Musial page, Wikipedia; Society for American Baseball Research (SABR), article on Stan Musial, by Jan Finkel; Sport Magazine, August, 1948, article "The Unusual Mr. Musial," by J. Roy Stockton; Stan Musial page of Baseball-Reference.com-splits: 1947, 1948; Freezing the Appendix, excerpts edited from Wikipedia; Desert Sun newspaper, article by Pete Donoven, from google search, Stan Musial; Baseball teams nicknames; google search.

BASEBALL'S CONTRIBUTION TO THE LEXICON

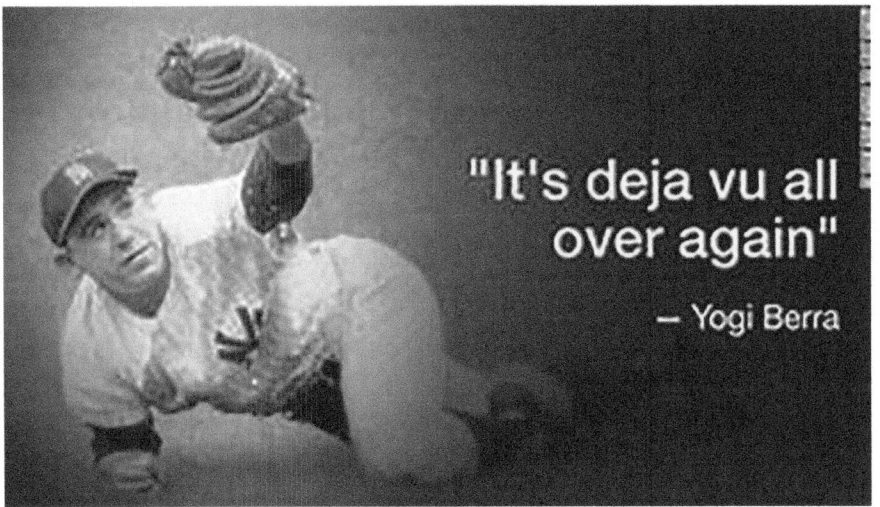

*Well—it's our game, that's the chief fact in connection with it: America's game; it has the snap, go, fling of the American atmosphere; it belongs as much to our institutions, fits into them as significantly as our Constitution's laws; is just as important in the sum total of our historic life----*Walt Whitman

The term *national pastime* was first recorded in 1856. But at that time the term really meant baseball as played by a new code of rules introduced by the New York Knickerbocker Ball Club in 1845. As the game grew increasingly popular, the expression *the national game* implied that baseball was the nation's favorite sport. The variation, *The National Pastime*, was introduced in the 1920's to indeed mean that baseball was the most popular sport in the country.

Arguments rage constantly about which sport really is the county's favorite; many feel basketball and football rank above baseball in popularity. But there can be no argument about which sport has produced the most phrases into the lexicon of the English language. This may be true because the real baseball fanatic in his or her zeal for the game literally hangs on every pitched ball and can recite statistics about the sport at the drop of a hat. For many, baseball becomes life in microcosm and, therefore, its terminology naturally spills over into the language in general.

A ball hit outside of the fair playing area in baseball has been called a *foul ball* since the 1860's. By the 1920's, the term was being used generally to describe any contemptible person. The great American word inventor, T. A. Dorgan is said to be the first person to use the expression in this extended sense. We've all known one or two "foul balls" in our lives!

The term *from out of left field* comes straight from the diamond also and means from out of nowhere unexpectedly. It can also mean unorthodox, weird, unconventional—even crazy. The reason for left field, as opposed to right or center field, is because *left* has long had negative associations of radical or eccentric behavior. Sorry, southpaws!

Getting to first base in baseball is the first step in scoring a run and it long ago suggested the slang expression *get to first base,* to take a successful first step or to begin well in anything. In relationships with the opposite sex, of course, "I didn't get to first base" means failure in the old mating game pursuit. Or, as Marilyn Monroe said to the gentleman who introduced her to Joe DiMaggio, "tell your ballplayer friend he *struck out!*" Obviously, Joe made a better impression the next time he *went up to bat* with the luscious MM. But, after September 1954, nobody used the word subway in Joltin Joe's presence ever again! [Ed. Note: Check out MM in the photo gallery!]

The term *home run* in baseball was first recorded in 1856, although a cricket term before it was used in baseball, and has come to mean a great accomplishment in any field. In bridge, a *grand slam* is the taking of all 13 tricks in a deal—and the phrase in that sense dates back to about 1895. By 1940, it became baseball's home run with the bases loaded, the sports ultimate home run. In general use, a *grand slam* is the quintessential peak of anything. During my wild and wooly bachelor days, the Grand Slam breakfast at Perkin's Pancake House was the apex of gustatory delights for me (life in the fast lane).

Baseball's *double play*, a play in which two put outs are made, was recorded as early as 1858 and has long since become a term Americans use when referring to any two accomplishments made at the same time.

By the end of the 19th century, *grandstanders* were players who played to the grandstand, by making easy catches look more difficult to better show off their skills. The term was soon applied to a show-off in any endeavor.

During the 1905 major league baseball season, the term *squeeze play* became consciously used when a batter tried to "squeeze in" a run by laying down a bunt in a no-out or one-out situation when there was a runner on third base. *Squeeze play* in American English also means to apply pressure on a person in order to gain an advantage or force compliance in a specific situation.

To surprise someone in a negative way, deceive or mislead, or ask a tricky question is to *throw someone a curve*. Of course, the expression has its roots in the curve pitch of baseball, which comes directly toward the batter and then breaks away, often surprising him. It is not an optical illusion as some misguided physicists once claimed. They never batted against Bob Feller, Sad Sam Jones, Bert Blyleven, Sal Maglie, Dwight Gooden or Adam Wainwright (just ask Carlos Beltran!).

The term *Screwball* can be traced back to the days of the New York Giants lefthander, Carl "King Carl" Hubbell, in the early '30s, when he introduced the left-handed pitch that corkscrewed crazily as it approached the batter. It was inevitably compared with an unpredictable, erratic, eccentric person, helped by the expression "he has a screw loose" common in the 1860s. (Actually, the first famous screwball was thrown by another legendary Giants pitcher some 30 years earlier. The immortal Christy Mathewson threw the same pitch right-handed but called it a *fadeaway*.)

In 1902, the term *pinch hitter* came into use to indicate a player who bats in a pinch for someone else. The expression has wide general use for any substitute or understudy in any endeavor. There are others: *A ballpark figure*-an estimate; *batting a thousand*-maintaining a perfect record; *play hardball*-extreme measures to ensure success.

Baseball fan or not, I guarantee the game has had some influence on the way you speak, like it or not!

[Ed. Note: Here's a few others from Bill Schaefer that have become part of the lexicon: "Can I have a rain check?" "I'll touch base with you," "It's a whole new ballgame," You're definitely out of your league," "You're really off-base with that comment."]

October 7, 2020

Sources: Baseball: A History of America's Favorite Game-George Vecsey; Baseball: An Illustrated History-Geoffrey C. Ward and Ken Burns; Google-Baseball Idioms for Everyday English; Wikipedia, The Seven Year Itch.

A MEMORABLE DAY AT YANKEE STADIUM

"Keller didn't look like he'd been scouted; he looked like he'd been trapped!" - Lefty Gomez, speaking of teammate Charlie "King Kong" Keller

My dad was a diehard New York Giants fan going back to his days growing up in Westfield, NJ. His favorite players were Christy Mathewson, Mel Ott, Carl Hubbell and Ross Youngs. But he also appreciated Ruth, Gehrig, DiMaggio, Berra et al. He took me to games at the Polo Grounds and Yankee Stadium beginning at the age of six. My fanatical attachment to the Giants developed a couple of years later.

It was a perfect Sunday in June, 1946. The war was over and many of the greats of the game were back in action, so we decided it would be a good idea to make the trip to 161st St. in the Bronx to catch the Yankees/Cleveland Indians twin bill. Everything was wonderful until we got to the Stadium and walked into a total mob scene! (Official attendance that day, June 9, was 66,545). I'll never forget looking far back into the deepest recesses of the lower grandstand and seeing the crowd three deep behind the railing of the last row.

The situation was hopeless and I wanted to get the heck out of there…as a little kid I was getting claustrophobic! I begged my dad to take me to one of the movie houses on 42nd St. so we could catch a double feature. The movies shown were a few years old but usually worth seeing. The year before, when the Giants were rained out, we saw "The Sea Wolf" with Edward G. Robinson as an unforgettably cruel ship's captain. I loved Robinson. Maybe we'd catch another great second run movie. But my dad was adamant, "Somehow, I think you will be the means of us getting good seats, he said matter-of-factly." By now, I may have whined a little and mumbled a prayer that this guy would please come to his senses.

Suddenly, as if a wand had been waved, a well-dressed "important" looking man was standing near a concession stand about 15 feet away. My dad instinctively walked over and said, "Excuse me, sir, but I brought my little boy 25 miles to see the Yankees play. Could you possibly be able to help us find two seats?" Remarkably, the gentleman reached into the vest pocket of his suit jacket and produced two tickets. We were flabbergasted when the usher led us to field boxes right next to the Yankee dugout! Now, you may be tempted to blurt out, "C'mon, Schaefer, what's the punch line to this dumb joke?" As they say, truth is stranger than fiction. And the stranger in question was none other than newly hired publicity chief/traveling secretary for the New York Yankees, Red Patterson. My father said, "See, I told you that you'd be…" I interrupted, "Yeah, but how did you know?" "Just a hunch" he replied, with a wry smile playing about his lips. I didn't want to go to the movies anymore.

Once we got settled in, a whole new world surrounded us. The vast expanses of the magnificent Yankee Stadium, beautifully manicured infield, lush green grass as far as the eye could see--and a cloudless summer sky. Plus, the vendors were all over us…"Hey scorecard heah… hey ice cream here…hot frank in a roll heah…ice cold beer here… seegars, cigarettes, candy here!" I probably lapped up half-a-dozen ice creams during the course of the afternoon. No more suffocating crowd. I was in my glory!

The Bronx Bombers split the double-header but I only remember the close up famous faces and the pinstripe uniforms as the players charged into the dugout. "That's "King Kong" Keller! I exclaimed. He had been described thusly: *with eyebrows that had been borrowed from a passing lowlands gorilla*. Lefty Gomez once said, "Keller didn't look like he'd been scouted; he looked like he'd been trapped."

Tommy Henrich seemed to have a permanent, pleasant half smile. Bob Feller rendered this assessment of Old Reliable, "Tough to strike out. Good clutch hitter. And it seemed he was always looking for the pitch I was delivering."

Bill Dickey was impressive, rangy for a catcher, and four years removed from giving a notably natural performance in the 1942 film, "The Pride of the Yankees." Speaking at spring training in '29, Miller Huggins spoke glowingly of the future HOF Yankee backstop, "This boy will be better than all of them (catchers)." When we saw Dickey behind the plate in 1946, little did we know we were watching him catch in his final major league season.

Joe DiMaggio had an aura about him. His feet never really seemed to touch the ground. During the 1938 All-Star game, Carl Hubbell captured The Yankee Clipper's ethereal quality, "Sure, I've faced great hitters but somehow you don't get the same feeling when they're at the plate as when Joe D. comes up."

Deep into the second game, I had an opportunity to absolutely cap off the day. Suddenly, a foul ball trickled right near our seats. In those days, nobody threw baseballs back into the stands. But they weren't as strict about fans quickly stepping over the small field railing to scoop up a prized white spheroid. My father tried his best, "Go on, Billy, climb over and get the ball!" I hesitated. He tried again, "Go on!" I just got over the rail when, out of nowhere; a long-legged ball boy swooped in and grabbed the ball. He wasn't about to relinquish the baseball to the poor little kid standing there, empty handed and slightly embarrassed. He who hesitates…

But, like I said at the beginning, it was, indeed, a memorable day at Yankee Stadium.

February 25, 2022

Sources: Yankee schedule almanac, 1946; box score, Yankees/Indians, June 9, 1946; specific quotes derived from 1946 almanac, New York Yankees.

THE TURBULENT LIFE OF HARRY "THE HAT" WALKER

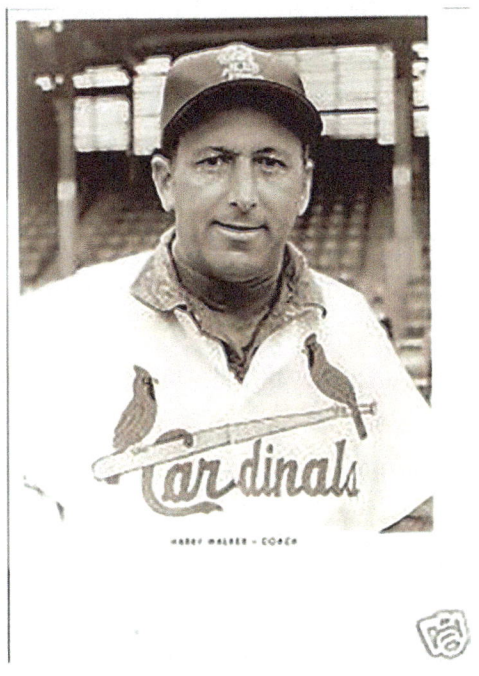

"He backs out of the batter's box. Cap off, cap on, tap left foot with bat, cap off again, tap right foot with bat, cap on again, adjust cap with left hand, cap off again, rub sleeve across face, cap on again, adjust cap with right hand, tap foot."-unnamed writer

"I relax my muscles, fix my hat and my hair...and maybe get the pitcher and catcher upset a little"-Harry Walker

Harry Walker won the National League batting crown with a .363 batting average, in 1947. And folks were flocking to see the year's biggest grossing movie, Forever Amber. But '47 stands out for me because it marked the first full year of my baseball fanaticism.

That year Walker also led the league in triples with 16 and an OBP of .436. He was a fine center fielder perfecting a sliding-on-his-knees catch, courtesy of the great Terry Moore's tutelage. However, he delivered but one home run and knocked in only 41 runs. Management frowned upon such a dearth of power and used it unfairly against "The Hat" in contract negotiations. (Walker at 6'2" 180 had a lefty power stroke in the minors but was advised to swing a heavier bat and slap the ball the opposite way to survive in the big leagues. He batted .296 for his 11 year career with just 10 homers.)

The contrast from the previous year was stark. He hit only .237 in 1946, returning from the service. In fact, Walker had an anemic .200 average for the Cardinals in his first 10 games of '47, when he was promptly dealt to the Phillies for Round Ron Northey. He then proceeded to spray the ball all over the National League at a .371 clip the rest of the way. He was the only player in National League history to win a batting title playing for two teams.

My dad mentioned that New York sports writer Dick Young noticed the official scorer at Shibe Park was awarding Walker a hit on practically every ground ball he beat out, bobbled by an opposing infielder. Philadelphia did its part to keep Harry on top!

After leading baseball with a batting average 20 points higher than Ted Williams, who led the American League with .343, how would you like to hear the following comments when requesting a raise to $30,000? "Harry, you haven't shown me you're a great hitter," said GM Herb Pennock, peering over his glasses and shaking his head. President Bob Carpenter smiled condescendingly and put it this way: "No, Harry. You just go back to Alabama and think it over."

So Harry sat it out in Alabama for a while, then caved in a week into spring training 1948 and called Carpenter. He accepted a bad deal, reportedly $22,500. He hoped things would be financially brighter the following year.

"Just call me Hard-Luck Harry," once bemoaned Walker. During his career, he suffered a barrage of ailments that would choke a horse—from prickly heat to peritonitis and from metatarsal trouble to a burst appendix that nearly proved fatal. He was fired almost too often to account. He had his arm and ankle broken, a tooth knocked out and his shoulder shattered. Once he was hit in the Adam's apple and couldn't talk for two months. Another time he couldn't see for two days.

Following the Yankees' victory over the Cardinals in the 1943 World Series, Walker and teammate Alpha Brazle reported to the US Army for basic training at fort Riley Kansas. On a January morning in 1944, he complained about feeling "beyond awful." He was given pills at the dispensary but they didn't work. Harry begged Army medical personnel to put him in the hospital but was told he'd have to wait until morning. A fever mounted and raged through the night. He became delirious and raving and had to be restrained in a straitjacket. He was diagnosed with spinal meningitis. Only the new miracle drug penicillin saved Walker's life. Harry went on to win a bronze star for valor and the Purple Heart.

Harry William Walker drew his first breath in Pascagoula Mississippi, on September 22, 1918. His father (the original Dixie Walker) had pitched for the Washington Senators from 1909 to 1912. His brother Fred "Dixie" Walker became a beloved hero for the Brooklyn Dodgers, known as "The People's Cherce." They were the only brother combo in baseball history to each win a batting title. Dixie led the league in 1944, batting .357. He was eight years older than harry but the brothers maintained a touchingly warm, close relationship throughout their lives.

Enos Slaughter was the hero in the 1946 World Series, famously scoring from first on an apparent single in the eighth inning to win the final game, as the Cardinals defeated the Red Sox. But do you know who sliced that sinking line drive to left field? Yup, Harry Walker! "Harry the

Hat" went 7-17 in the '46 World Series and was a key cog for St. Louis. But you never hear his name mentioned.

Walker never drank alcohol or coffee but had bubbling-over nervous energy. The Hat Trick was not a showboat act, just his way of burning off that excess juice. But it annoyed the hell out of opposing players and umpires. In August of 1947, ump Beans Reardon halted a game twice to go through the same routine as Walker. Then he looked hard at Harry and said, "I just wanted to show you what a jackass you're making out of yourself." Walker only grinned and touched his cap.

After his playing career he managed the Cardinals in 1955, the Pirates 65-'67, and the Astros, '68-'72. Walker was loved by the fans but his assertive personality created conflict elsewhere. Tired of his rants about things political, Houston Astro's owner Judge Roy Hofheinz decided it was time for a change in 1973. Walker stayed in the organization as a scout. His nine-year managerial record flashed 630-604 on the ledger.

He was a masterful batting coach and according to a slumping first baseman, Bill White, "He absolutely saved my major league career." (and, by so doing, also saved an even better career in the Yankees broadcast booth).

Astros GM Spec Richardson remembered, "Some people didn't like Harry because he talked all the time. But if you listened to him, you learned a lot."

1978 saw The University of Alabama at Birmingham (UAB), 30 miles from his home in Leeds, hire him to create a varsity baseball program. A much mellower Walker was so successful that eight years later, his number 32 was the first UAB baseball jersey to be retired and he was elected to the Alabama Sports Hall of Fame in 1978.

Walker passed on peacefully on August 8, 1999, at the age of 80. He was survived by his wife, Dot, three daughters, and four grandchildren.

Harry summed up his life succinctly, "Baseball gave me the best of lives. The only thing I never had that I really wanted was a jet airplane."

October 30, 2022

Sources: Sport Magazine, July 1948; Harry Walker, The Hard-Luck Kid, by Stan Baumgartner. Harry Walker-Wikipedia; Harry Walker Baseball Reference.com; Society For American Baseball Research (SABR): Harry Walker, by Warren Corbett; The New York Times-Harry Walker, 80, is Dead-A Fidgeter With a Purpose, by Richard Goldstein.

FLASHBACKS... AND WHO'S ON FIRST (on *your* all-time team)?

"You take the first pick and I'll take the second and we'll come up even. For instance, if you say Mickey Mantle, I'll say Willie Mays; if you say Henry Aaron, I'll say Roberto Clemente. Besides, the choices will vary from day to day, depending on emotion and recollection."-Tom Seaver

"It's a mere moment in a man's life between an All-Star game and an old-timers game."-Vin Scully

There's nothing like it for a kid, getting his or her psyche wrapped around baseball and the home team for the first time. It's a joyous, thrilling, agonizing, gut-wrenching journey. You vow you're through with that miserable team until the next day's victory, and then the "hanging on every pitch" starts all over again. And, oh, those images branded on the brain, forever. Two stand out for me:

(1) Polo Grounds, 1947, Pittsburgh third baseman Frankie Gustine smashes a screaming line drive that Giants shortstop Buddy Kerr, with a tremendous leap, spears…with his bare hand!

(2) First time I saw Mickey Mantle, on TV, May 1951 at Yankee Stadium. The Mick executes a bad drag bunt, one quick hop to the pitcher who throws immediately to first base. The camera then pans to the bag, and Mantle is barely out - bang, bang! *Oh, my God, he was shot out of a cannon!*

And just as powerful is the passion we have for every all-time, all-star position favorite. Using an amazing book for a reference, titled, The Greatest Team of All Time, let me share some fascinating selections and insights from those involved at the highest level of the game. Here goes.

SIX HALL OF FAMERS SELECT THEIR BEST

HENRY AARON stated categorically, "There was never a pitcher I felt I couldn't get a hit off." Hammerin' Hank, who had more RBI and total bases than any player in history, picks Bob Gibson (RHP) and Sandy Koufax (LHP) as his two mound immortals. But he adds that Juan Marichal and Don Drysdale rivaled Gibson in the tough-to-hit category. "It's true I hit more home runs off Don Drysdale than any other player did. But there was a slew of other at-bats when he punished me."

Aaron has Musial, Mays, and Clemente comprising his star-studded outfield. Up the middle: Ernie Banks and Jackie Robinson. At the corners, Eddie Mathews and Gil Hodges. Behind the plate, Roy Campanella. "When he was healthy there was nobody better than Campy as a catcher and a hitter."

LUIS APARICIO was, perhaps, the greatest defensive shortstop in American League history. He leads all shortstops in games played and career assists. He also led the American League in stolen bases from '56-'64. Here's who Luis promotes as his best: Frank Robinson, Mickey

Mantle and Al Kaline patrolling the outfield. Around the horn, starting at third base, he likes Brooks Robinson, Tony Kubek, Bobby Richardson, and Vic Power, at first. For one big game, Aparicio gives the nod to Jim Palmer (RHP) and Dave McNally (LHP). And his catcher is Bill Freehan.

Luis says this about Frank Robinson, "He could beat you a hundred ways. When he didn't hit he'd steal a base or make a great catch, or kick a ball out of an infielder's glove. I don't know of anybody who ever played the game who was more of a force on the field."

JOHN BERTRAND "JOCKO" CONLON umpired in the National League from 1941-1965, and was elected to the Hall of Fame in 1974. The diminutive arbitrator cut quite a figure on the field, complete with a polka dot bow tie and a big balloon chest protector. Conlin was "a master psychologist who knew when to cajole, when to rebuff, and when to ignore." But don't curse him out, or you're gone." Durocher was king of the complainers and moaners," said Jocko. "We had many a run-in. But he was a first-class manager." Like Leo, Jackie Robinson was profane on the field, which irked Conlin. "Jackie was the most difficult ball player I ever dealt with as an umpire. He would never accept a decision."

Here's JBC's best team: Walter Johnson (RHP), Lefty Grove (LHP). Conlon said neither threw a curve, nor did either ever have a sore arm. At the hot corner, Pie Traynor is the choice, with Lou Gehrig anchoring first base. Through the center of the diamond, Gabby Hartnett (C), Honus Wagner (SS), Charlie Gehringer (2B), and Tris Speaker (CF), with Ty Cobb (LF) and Babe Ruth (RF) rounding out his all-star team.

JUDY JOHNSON was considered the best third baseman of his day in the Negro Leagues, topping a .400 BA in 1929. Johnson played for the 1935 champion Pittsburgh Crawfords, along with Josh Gibson, Cool Papa Bell, and Oscar Charleston. Judy proclaims, "It was maybe the best team ever, black or white. And Josh Gibson was the best hitter I ever saw."

Who's going to argue with him?

SOME CATCH!

MICKEY MANTLE combined the gifts of enormous power and the speed of Mercury, yet we'll never know how great he might have been had it not been for injuries and other extenuating circumstances. As it is, his stats still jump off the page. In twelve World Series, he set records for most home runs (18), RBI (40), runs scored (42), and walks (43). He said he swung as hard as he could on every pitch.

The Commerce Comet vouchsafed, "In picking a team, I only need two—Whitey Ford and Ted Williams. The others wouldn't much matter: we'd still beat most anybody." His most challenging hurler was Red Sox right-hander Dick Radatz. "I read in a Dallas newspaper, I faced him 66 times in my career and he struck me out 45 times. If he wasn't the toughest, I don't want to remember who was."

EARLY WYNN won 300 games, even. He said Yogi Berra was impossible for him. "He hit everything I threw, including one time I bounced a curve six feet in front of the plate and he slammed it for a double."

Well, it's time to go. But not before we present the final 1994 Greatest Team of All Time tally. It's still glorified hot stove stuff, 29 years ago. But it does involve the men who grappled between the white lines, many of whom qualified as true fanatics.

First base: Lou Gehrig was named by more than half of his contemporaries.

Second base: Jackie Robinson was chosen by one fewer respondent than Charlie Gehringer, but captured a higher percentage of his contemporaries.

Third base: Brooks Robinson beats Pie Traynor by one slice.

Shortstop: Honus Wagner was the unanimous choice of his contemporaries.

Outfield: Ty Cobb was selected by almost everyone who played with or against him.

Outfield: Willie Mays was picked for 25 lineups, the most of anyone.

Outfield: Babe Ruth trails only Mays in his number of lineup inclusions.

Catcher: Dead heat on a merry-go-round with Bench and Campanella tied at 11 selections. But Johnny wins the contemporary game.

RHP: Walter Johnson over Bob Gibson in a photo finish—with Walter's entries representing a higher percentage of those who faced him.

LHP: Sandy Koufax with 21 likes, second only to Willie Mays' 25 among all players.

Looks like a pretty good group to me, what do you think?

January 11, 2023

Sources: *"The Greatest Team of All Time,"* compiled by Nicholas Acocella and Donald Dewey, 1994; SABR article, Jocko Conlon, by Rodney Johnson; NY Giants schedule almanac, 1947; quotes online re All-Star baseball; Luis Aparicio, Baseball reference.

SNAP SHOTS FROM A GIANTS FAN, THROUGH A SURREAL SEASON

On a sultry August afternoon in 1950, from our perch in the Polo Grounds upper deck, my father and I watched Eddie Stanky drill an apparent single to right field. But why was Eddie running for his life? Then we saw Carl Furillo swoop in from his shallow position in right, scoop the ball and unleash a missile to Gil Hodges at first base! Stanky was out by an eyelash, but Hodges couldn't hold the Reading Rifle's powerful throw.

Stanky's awareness and hustle characterized Leo Durocher's "My kind of team."

That year, the Giants were 36-46 on July 19. They then won 17 of 18 and went 50-22 to close out the season! There were great expectations for 1951.

Larry Jansen shut out the Braves, 4-0, on opening day in Boston, April 17. After a loss, they won the first game of a Patriots' Day double header, as General Douglas MacArthur, back from Korea, was delivering his "Old Soldiers Never Die" speech.

A gut wrenching defeat that night began an 11 game losing streak.

The club stood 2-12 on April 29. One Giants fan prayed, "Lord, I asked for a dream season. I'd thank you not to give me a nightmare!"

The team turned on a dime and won 40 of their next 60 games. A crucial meeting loomed with the dodgers, on the fourth of July.

Ebbets Field, with its Dodger Sym-Phony, 40-foot right field screen, and Gladys Gooding at the organ, was at once charming and daunting. Trading for Andy Pafko in June made Brooklyn a total wrecking crew, especially in that cozy ball yard.

Before the July showdown...

Monte Irvin simply could not catch the ball at first base and went back to the outfield. Whitey Lockman took over on May 21.

Four days later, the Giants brought up a just turned 20-year-old from their Minneapolis farm. He had devastated the American Association with a .477 batting average, and played center field like he invented the position.

Willie Mays promptly went 0-12 against the Phillies and then launched a rocket over the roof at the Polo grounds against the great Warren Spahn-followed by another 0-13. He was bludgeoning baseballs directly into opposing gloves. Then the hits started to fall.

SOME CATCH!

In early June, Leo Durocher replaced Herman Franks in the third base coaching box. Franks was so cautious he thought twice before waving a runner around third base on a homerun.

My dad and I wanted a sweep in the big series. That would put us only a game and a half behind the first place Dodgers. Instead, *we* got swept! A twin shocker on the fourth, and the Dodgers pulled ahead by 7 1/2 games with a win on Thursday, July 5. We were devastated. The first pennant since Bill Terry managed the Giants in 1937, now seemed a pipe dream.

From the end of June, through the first game of a double header on August 11, Brooklyn went 29-10. A headline appeared on the back page of the Daily News: **BUMS (YAWN) WIN AGAIN.**

Brooklyn was breezing with a 13 1/2 game lead. The Giants were blanked by Phillies ace Robin Roberts and manager Eddie Sawyer predicted his team would leapfrog the Giants into second place.

Somehow, though, I still had hope. Durocher could drive a team like no other. And Bobby Thomson, now playing third base, was coming off a blistering July-.345 with 11 homers and 30 RBI!

In the first of a pair on Sunday, August 12, Monte Irvin lofted a high drive that kissed off the right field roof just inside the foul pole, for a three run homer. Phillies lefthander Jocko Thompson was incensed, "I had Irvin struck out. He barely flicked the ball, right out of Andy Seminick's mitt!" The Jints won 3-2, behind Sal Maglie.

Bobby Thomson drove in both runs for a 2-1 victory in the second game.

Magic was in the air.

Flashes…to the finish line:

- On August 15, Billy Cox was poised at third with the game knotted at one. Willie Mays sped into medium right center to grab Carl Furillo's fly ball--then whirled 180 degrees, releasing an amazing strike to Wes Westrum! A sliding Cox bounced off the sturdy Giants catcher into his waiting tag. Wes then insured the Giants 5th straight win with a two run homer off Ralph Branca.

- The Brooks were swept the next day. Coming into town, they had beaten the Giants 12 of 15 games.

- On Sunday, August 26, my Dad and I were on the edge of our seats, in the horseshoe shaped park, as our heroes gunned for 13 straight facing the Cubs, in the first of two. Suddenly, a huge roar erupted--a big **8** appeared on the scoreboard in the Pittsburgh seventh! The Pirates went on to edge Brooklyn 12-11. The Giants prevailed 5-4 and the lead was six!

- After a second double header sweep on Monday, 16 straight wins cut the Dodger margin to five games!

The following afternoon, a drained Durocher crew wilted against Howie Pollet and the Pirates, 2-0.

Mind bogglers…

Sunday, September 9th saw the Giants play the Dodgers for the final time, at Ebbets Field. The lead was 6 1/2 games. With the Giants leading 2-1 in the Brooklyn eighth and Jackie Robinson on third, Andy Pafko exploded out of his rocking chair crouch and smashed a bullet ticketed for the left field corner. Bobby Thomson miraculously backhanded the drive on the short hop, tagged Robinson sliding back to third and fired to first, to Whitey Lockman, completing an incredible double play! A weary Sal Maglie preserved a precious 2-1 victory."

The magnitude of that play, with only 16 games remaining, was expressed by Dick Young in Monday's Daily News: "*If by some miracle the Giants go on to snag the NL flag, Giants fans will not remember Monte Irvin's home run or that Sal Maglie won his 20th. They will remember Bobby Thomson's game saving play*" He was so right!

SOME CATCH!

The Giants blazed down the stretch, winning 12 of their final 13 games. On the last day of the regular season, September 30th, masterful Larry Jansen beat the Braves 3-2, to go 22-11. They now led Brooklyn by a half game, having won 37 of 44 games!

Meanwhile, in Philadelphia, the Dodgers were deadlocked in the bottom of the 13th when Jackie Robinson made an impossible diving catch of an Eddie Waitkus looper in short center field, to forestall oblivion. He then slugged a homerun in the top of the 14th to win it, 9-8! Robinson was the greatest competitor I ever saw.

The breathless season went non-stop to Flatbush the next day for the first playoff game. Jim Hearn handcuffed the Dodgers 3-1. Often obscured is Bobby Thomson's game winning, two run homer in the fourth inning… victimizing Ralph Branca!

On Tuesday, the baseball gods mercifully provided a respite from the relentless pressure with a 10-0 Dodger drubbing at the Polo Grounds, behind a brilliant Clem Labine.

October 3 was showdown time at Coogan's Bluff. I got home from school to join my dad as the eighth inning unfolded. We watched in horror as Bobby Thomson was handcuffed twice by tough infield hits, leading to three Dodger runs and a 4-1 lead. Don Newcombe looked invincible in the Giants home half. Jansen, replacing Maglie, retired Brooklyn, in order, in the ninth.

Alvin Dark and Don Mueller opened the Giants 9th with singles. Then Irvin popped out. Our hearts sank. Monte was our big gun. But Whitey Lockman sliced a patented Lockman opposite field double to left, scoring Dark. Wthout eye-popping statistics, Whitey was one of the best clutch hitters I ever saw, always coming through for Giants fans. Mueller pulled a tendon in his ankle and left on a stretcher, replaced by pinch runner Clint Hartung. Branca relieved Newcombe, and faced Bobby Thomson.

The Stage Was Set…

After a strike, Ralph threw a second fastball inside. Thomson swung hard and smote a sinking line drive blur into the lower deck of the left field stands! "The Shot Heard 'Round the World" won the pennant for New York and Jansen earned win number 23, equaling Sal Maglie.

In 1966, a young broadcaster interviewed Thomson in his Watchung, NJ home. He told me, "In 1951, I was lightening quick getting around on the inside fastball. They couldn't throw it past me."

Had the injured MVP Roy Campenella been behind the plate in that third playoff game instead of Rube Walker, do you think Thomson would have gotten two consecutive fast balls on the inside part of the plate?

The second yielded Giants fans the greatest possible joy…and brought Dodger fans unthinkable desolation.

PS A few additional notes on the season and the historic playoff game:

(1) Homeplate umpire Lou Jorda said in a post game interview, "Thomson didn't get the good part of his bat on the ball." Yes, Bobby hit it toward the end of the bat, but got enough wood, combined with a great swing, to send a screaming clout into the lower left field seats.

(2) Thomson emphasized, "I'm proud of my swing on the ball. Look at the pictures and notice the follow through." He's right-a classic swing. Bob almost tomahawked the slightly high fastball and lashed it with heavy topspin-a "topped" liner-headed in a white flash toward the green left field wall. That's why a helpless Ralph Branca kept yelling from the mound, "Sink, sink!"

(3) The homer went over the 16 foot wall, just to the left of the 315 foot sign. According to Josh Prager, author of The Echoing Green, the ball traveled approximately 345 feet.

(4) No, it wouldn't have been a homer in any other ball park. But Thomson took what they gave him and drove one of the few home runs into the left field stands at the Polo Grounds, at such a low trajectory, that it didn't hit the upper deck overhang.

(5) Mrs. John McGraw attended the October 3 playoff game and told reporters, "When Ralph came in, I thought we had a chance." Branca was a good pitcher and a fine man with a great heart. But he had the unforunate propensity to yield the big four bagger late in games.

(6) So much has been discussed about the Giants' sign stealing that year, which was, indeed, a fact. But it is the contention of many that it had nothing to do with the outcome.

(7) Durocher's gang picked off pitching signs from July 20th, but curiously the team batting average was higher before that date, than after the fourth week of July. Two of the Giants best clutch hitters, Monte Irvin and Whitey Lockman, did not want the signs.

(8) The team went on their 16 game winning streak August 12. Counting the first playoff game at Ebbets Field, they went 38-7. They were 20-3 at home. But they copped 18 of 22 on the road. That's .818 baseball with no stolen signs!

(9) Robin Roberts shut them out 4-0 at the PG on August 11. Roberts gave up an average of 27 home runs per season and led the league four consecutive years in home runs allowed. So, if knowing Robin's pitches in advance was such an advantage, you'd think at least two or three would have left the park, right?

(10) Howie Pollet shut them out to snap the 16 game streak on August 28, in New York. And Clem Labine Blanked the Gians 10-0 on October 2, at Coogan's Bluff. So much for stealing their pitches.

(11) Finally, the Giants batters had approximately 2.5 seconds to get the stolen sign and get ready for the pitch. Talk about pressure. How about being so geared up for the pitch, that the over anxious hitter might swing too hard and pop out, instead of waiting the extra split second and clocking a drive over the wall? Or, the pitch is so good even Ted Williams, on his best day, would have watched it sail into the catcher's mitt. Or, the pitcher crosses everybody up and throws a different pitch?

In addition to timely hitting, the Giants won with airtight pitching down the stretch. Their 3.48 staff ERA easily topped the National League.

And, by the way, according to writer, Scott Ferkovich, "When Thomson connected no one was more delighted than rookie Willie Mays, next up in the on-deck circle. He later admitted he was terrified to bat in such a pressure packed situation."

May 5, 2020

THE GREAT BASEBALL NAME GAME: "VINEGAR BEND" MIZELL

Part of the lore and lure of baseball are the wonderfully screwy names of baseball players. There was: Round Ron Northey, Erv "Four Sack" Dusak, Blue Moon Odom, Whitey Wietelmann, Monk Dubiel, Hooks Wiltse, The Hondo Hurricane, Three Finger Brown, Stubby Clap, Mysterious Walker, Boots Poffenberger, Orval Overall, Possum Whitted, The Splendid Splinter, Stan The Man, Wahoo Sam Crawford, Hugh High, Willie Puddin' Head Jones…not to mention Pretzels Puzzullo, Peanuts Lowry and Cookie Lavagetto!

But let's spotlight Wilmer David "Vinegar Bend" Mizell. He was born in Leaksville Mississippi, August 13, 1930. But the tiny unincorporated census-designated place in Washington County, Alabama, known as

Vinegar Bend, was on the family's residence mail route. Thus, Vinegar Bend was recorded as his birthplace and he was nicknamed for the community. The little "town" (under 200 people) got its name when a train passing through careened off the tracks and spilled its load of vinegar there.

THE EARLY YEARS

Walter Mizell died when Wilmer was only two-years-old. His mom became seriously ill soon thereafter, so he was raised by his grandmother and uncle. Young Wilmer took to throwing a baseball right away but had a crazy motion and was so wild his brother couldn't play catch with him. He improved his control by throwing at a knothole in the side of the family's smokehouse until he knocked the door down with his powerful arm.

Vinegar Bend started playing organized ball when he was 16 and pitched in Sunday leagues near his adopted home. A year later he attended a St. Louis Cardinals tryout camp in Biloxi, Mississippi. Buddy Lewis, a Cardinals scout, was impressed and came back the following spring on Mizell's high-school graduation day to watch the big left-hander pitch again. Having just taken a dip in a nearby swimming hole, Mizell showed up barefoot and, sans any footwear whatever, proceeded to wow the scout with a fastball that jumped all over the place. Lewis offered to sign him after graduation for $500. In rapid-fire succession, Wilmer received his diploma, signed his contract, and left on a train for Georgia after the graduation- without even returning home from the ceremony!

In 1949, Vinegar Bend was first assigned to Albany, Georgia, of the Class D GeorgiaFlorida League. On his very first pitch, he pulled a Ryne Duren, throwing the ball 20 feet over the backstop. But Mizell settled down, going 12-3 with a 1.98 ERA, striking out 175 batters in 141 innings as Albany went on to win the league pennant. A Westfield, NJ high school all-star pitcher faced Mizell in those early days and told me, "all you saw was Mizell's big right leg go up in the air, the left hand comes out of his mitt…then you heard the ball smack into the catcher's glove." This jibes with teammate Ken Boyer's comment, "the guy shows you his glove, his rear, and somebody tells you it's a strike."

It was on to Winston-Salem of the Class B Carolina League, in 1950, where Mizell dominated and pitched the team to a championship, striking out 227 in 207 innings. The next year and final stop before St. Louis, saw him join the Houston Buffaloes--where Vinegar Bend led the Texas League with 257 K's and a sparkling 1.96 ERA.

ON TO THE MAJORS

Wilmer Mizell was primed and ready for the St. Louis Cardinals in 1952 and their new manager, Eddie Stanky. The Redbirds could hit, with Enos Slaughter and Stan Musial in the middle of the lineup but needed bolstering on the mound. Vinegar Bend was thought to be an exciting addition.

In '52, major league attendance had plummeted for the second year in a row. Many thought television was the culprit. Boston would lose the Braves to Milwaukee in 1953. But New York still had three dominant baseball teams and fans in the tristate area were more than happy.

As Charles Dickens profoundly observed, "it was the best of times, it was the worst of times." Gas was 25 cents a gallon, the airbag was invented, a charismatic five-star general won a landslide presidential victory, and Emmett Ashford became the first African-American umpire in organized baseball.

However, the Korean War was still raging and a stark fear of poliomyelitis gripped the nation, with no vaccine in sight.

During the Cardinals' spring training in 1952, sportswriter Red Smith described Vinegar Bend Mizell as a "left-handed Dizzy Dean," with "a fluid, easy motion and a singing fastball." He led the league with 6.9 strikeouts per nine innings pitched, but allowed a league-leading 103 walks in 190 innings. With better command he would have improved on his 10-8 record and 3.65 ERA.

In 1953, he became a 13 game-winner against 11 losses with a tidy 3.49 ERA, but the 6-foot-3- in. Mizell walked a whopping 114 in 224 innings. He topped the league again with nearly seven strikeouts per nine innings. (Just to keep things in perspective, last year Gerrit Cole led the majors with 13.82 whiffs per nine innings. The average fastball when Mizell pitched was reported to be just a tad over 90 mph. Last year it was 93.4).

At the end of the season, after two deferments, the draft caught up with the big lefty and he spent the next two years in the army. Back on the mound for the Cards, in 1956, Vinegar Bend followed a familiar pattern of mediocrity sprinkled with brilliance, over the years to come.

But there were two distinct bright spots. In 1959 Mizell had a fine first half: 9-3, with a 3.05 ERA. This gave the jumbo southpaw a birth on the rosters of both National League All-Star squads, as two showcase games were played that year. And in 1960, Vinegar Bend was traded to the Pirates, in essence, for Julian Javier. Mizell was a key cog in the Pirates pennant run, going 13-5 with a nifty 3.12 ERA and a stretch of 30 consecutive scoreless innings. Javier became a mainstay at second base for St. Louis, for the next dozen years.

In his only start in the classic 1960 World Series, a "storybook" version might spin a tale he dominated the mighty Yankees, shutting them out with 13 strikeouts. But, alas, our boy lasted only a third of an inning and gave up four runs, on three hits and one walk. The Yankees won, 10-0.

Mizell endured his least effective full season in 1961, going 7-10 with a 5.04 ERA and was traded to the brand-new Mets the next year for first baseman Jim Marshall on May 7, 1962. Ironically, Vinegar Bend had defeated his new team before the trade, in his first start of the season, to post his 100th win and final major league victory. The Mets released him on August 4th and the books closed with Wilmer finishing his big league career with a record of 100-98, and a 3.85 ERA.

BEYOND THE WHITE LINES

After playing baseball, the affable Mizell took a crack at baseball broadcasting, became an executive for the Pepsi-Cola Company, and, in 1968, he was elected to the US House of representatives from North Carolina. A Republican, Vinegar Bend spent three terms in the House before being defeated in 1974, a victim of the Watergate scandal.

Mizell was ultra-conservative and scored a zero rating by the ADA (Americans for Democratic Action). That score indicated a total lack of support for any liberal legislation! He gently chided House Minority Leader Gerald Ford for being a dull speaker, with a flat monotone delivery. Ford did not take umbrage, it was impossible to get mad at the ex-pitcher who looked like Li'l Abner. In 1975, President Ford named Mizell the assistant Secretary of Commerce for economic development.

Vinegar Bend charmed everyone with his Southern drawl and country-boy wit, "The worst that happened to us back home in Vinegar Bend was the time we had the fire. It started in the bathroom. Fortunately, we were able to put it out before it reached the house."

No drugs, no-nonsense, successful in marriage, adored by his two sons and grandchildren, Wilmer David Vinegar Bend Mizell passed away on February 21, 1999, at the age of 68. With a big smile and a perennial effervescence, he was certainly made to work well in the world.

July 15, 2020

Sources: Vinegar Bend Mizell, Society for American Baseball Research Bioproject; Wilmer Mizell-Wikipedia page; NY Times Wilmer Mizell Obituary; *Wilmer David Mizell: The Buff from Vinegar Bend!*

ANOTHER EDITION OF BASEBALL'S FORGOTTEN STARS: "PISTOL" PETE REISER

"The only ballplayer I ever saw who was better than Willie Mays"- Leo Durocher

As a kid, the pint sized Reiser would roam around the neighborhood with a pair of toy six-shooters holstered to his belt, possessing a lightning fast draw with either hand. You see, the little fella was ambidextrous. The latter would serve him well at the major league level.

SOME CATCH!

A talented pitcher in his own right, Reiser's dad pitched to his young son at nearly full throttle, amazed the boy could hit most of his pitches. Pete's older brother, Mike, often brought him to play in his sandlot games, thus forcing him to "play up" in competition with older kids.

Pete was a natural athlete but as he matured into his compact 5' 11" 185 pound frame, baseball was the game Reiser pursued at William Beaumont High School as the team's shortstop. He ran like a cheetah, clocking 9.8 seconds in the 100 yard dash, with a rifle arm and a bat that exploded line drives all over the field from both sides of the plate. Plus, Pete believed he could catch anything hit in his direction. This, unfortunately, would prove a problem later on.

(Reiser actually snuck into a St. Louis Cardinal tryout at the age of 15 and proceeded to outperform more than 800 other boys. Cardinal scout, Charlie Barrett, confessed St. Louis had their eye on the lad since grammar school and wanted to keep him a secret)

He was signed by the Cardinals in 1937, after high school, and played shortstop for two Class D teams in Louisiana and Arkansas. Then, in 1938, Commissioner Kenesaw Mountain Landis ruled the Branch Rickey St. Louis "farm system" tied up so many young players that it went against the interest of baseball. Dozens of players were cut loose and then dispersed to other teams. The Mahatma leveled a keen eye on one of those players—Pete Reiser.

Rickey and former colleague Larry MacPhail, now the Dodger's honcho, cooked up a rather nefarious scheme whereby Brooklyn signed Reiser for a mere $100 and shipped him to a Wisconsin Class D league team. Pete would then be traded back to the Cardinals before the 1939 season.

Reiser was now batting left-handed exclusively to take advantage of his speed. On a blazing hot first day of spring training in '39, Leo asked Pete to play shortstop. Over the next three games, Reiser made 11 trips to the plate, producing three walks, four singles, and four home runs-they literally couldn't get him out! Durocher announced Pistol Pete would be his opening day shortstop. Branch Rickey read the papers and called MacPhail screaming about a double cross. MacPhail was then forced to instruct a bewildered and furious Durocher to option his young star to Class A Elmira in upstate New York.

But Reiser remained in the Brooklyn organization and by July, 1940, he was a Dodger and hit a solid .293 in 58 games.

A season played under the encroaching shadows of World War 11, 1941 was arguably the most exciting season ever. Joltin' Joe hit in 56 straight games, Teddy Ballgame batted .406 and the pivotal game of the World Series was won after the last out was called.

The Dodgers hadn't won a championship since 1920 and were a veritable laughing stock for 18 years. Then, with the hiring of Larry MacPhail, and the arrival of Pete Reiser, things changed dramatically.

Pistol Pete hit the ground running in '41. He established himself in centerfield between vets Joe Medwick and Dixie Walker and tore it up right out of the gate. He fielded like a demon, won the batting title (.343), led in doubles (39), triples (17), runs scored (117) and slugging percentage (.558). He also had a league leading OPS+ of 164 and finished a close second to teammate Dolph Camilli in voting for NL MVP.

The Dodgers won the pennant beating the Cards in a wild topsy-turvy race to the finish. They lost the WS to the Yankees in five games. The real story, however, was game four. The first three were decided by one run as Brooklyn trailed two games to one. But Reiser's fifth-inning two-run homer gave the Dodgers a 4-3 lead that held with two out in the ninth and two strikes on Tommy Henrich. Hugh Casey threw Old Reliable, "The greatest, craziest curve I ever saw. Not a spitter. I couldn't hold up. But strangely I was thinking if I'm having so much trouble with this pitch maybe Mikey Owen will too." Sure enough, Owen couldn't hold the ball. Henrich was safe at first and the flood gates opened. The Yankees won 7-4 and closed out the Series the next day.

SOME CATCH!

Reiser was even better in 1942. He was batting .356 on July 18 and his great friend, Pee Wee Reese was having a fine year also. Sports writers were calling them The Gold Dust Twins. Then on July 19, as the first place Dodgers were squaring off against the second place Cardinals at Sportsman's Park, Enos Slaughter scorched a rising line drive to dead center. Reiser, off with the crack of the bat, corralled the ball in full stride and, like a Japanese kamikaze pilot, crashed full speed into the concrete wall, the baseball jarring loose. Miraculously, Reiser managed to pick up the ball and throw to cutoff man Reese, who fired home-but too late to get Slaughter who circled the bases with the winning run.

Reiser lay on the field motionless staring skyward, blood trickling from his ears. Durocher cried when he saw him. The hospital diagnosis was a separated shoulder, severely bruised skull and a possible brain injury. Pete returned to the field way too soon and was never the same again, battling fits of vertigo. He batted .310 for the season but only .244 from July 25 to season's end. Still, the Dodgers were 10 games ahead of the Cards on August fifth and won 104 games. But St. Louis closed with a scintillating run of 43-9 to win 106-and the pennant!

Reiser enlisted in 1943 and served in the Army, returning to the Dodgers in 1946. A separated right shoulder sustained in a service game hampered his throwing and curtailed his power, but he could still motor and led the league with 34 thefts, including a record seven steals of home plate!

Historic 1947 saw Jackie Robinson spark the Dodgers to a pennant, while Reiser was having another injury riddled season. His bat rejuvenated to a nice .309 in 110 games but fans remembered another devastating encounter with the center field wall at Ebbets Field, with Brooklyn hosting the Pirates. A brilliant grab of a Culley Rikard bullet sent Reiser smashing violently into the concrete. He somehow held onto the ball, but again suffered a severely bruised skull. He lay in a hospital bed, hovering between life and death for five days, and was given last rites.

He was now a part time, oft injured player, and after the '48 season Pete asked Rickey to trade him. Branch obliged and Reiser spent time with the Braves, then was reunited with Rickey in Pittsburgh, briefly, and finally called it a playing career in Cleveland in 1952. His 10 year major league record showed a .295 batting average and an OPS+ of 128. Not bad, but a shadow of what might have been.

Pete joined Walter Alston's staff in 1960 and was instrumental in Maury Wills' achieving 104 steals in 1962, breaking Ty Cobb's record.

Most major league walls were padded by the early 50's thanks to Pete Reiser. He was carried off on a stretcher11 times. Five of those times he was unconscious.

A reporter asked if things might have been different had Pete been more cautious in his pursuit of fly balls. Reiser replied, "Never. It was my way of playing. If I hadn't played that way I wouldn't even have been whatever I was. God gave me those legs and the speed, and when they took me into the walls that's the way it had to be."

"My candle burns at both ends; It will not last the night; But ah, my foes, and oh my friends—it gives a lovely light!"

March 23, 2022

Sources: Edna St. Vincent Millay, First Fig; bleacher report.com; ladodgertalk.com; Maury Wills baseball ref; Pete Reiser baseball ref; '41 Dodger sched almanac; '42 Cardinal sched almanac; SABR article, Pete Reiser, by Mark Stewart.

MEL OTT—THE BIGGEST LITTLE GIANT

"Every time I sign a ball, and there must have been thousands, I thank my luck that I wasn't born Coveleski or Wamsganss or Peckinpaugh." -Mel Ott

Bill Schaefer Recalls the Day...

My dad and I were plopped comfortably in our favorite upper deck seats at the Polo Grounds, just to the left of home plate. It was the home eighth, first game of a twin bill, on July 11, 1947, with the Giants trailing the Cardinals 4-3. Our favorites were an exciting team that would belt a record 221 round-trippers, but would also allow runs by the bushel.

Now, with two out, the summer air was pierced by Polo Grounds PA announcer, Jim Gory, "Attention please, ladies and gentlemen, for the Giants, now batting for Larry Jansen, number 4, Mel Ott." Manager Mel was only making cameo appearances now due to deteriorating vision.

Ott had clubbed his historic 511th and final career homer the year before on opening day at Coogan's Bluff, victimizing Phillies left-hander Oscar Judd. A knee injury suffered the very next afternoon short-circuited his '46 season. He batted an embarrassing .074, going 5-for-68. As the Hall of Fame powerhouse admitted, "That year my eyesight started to betray me, the ball began to jump in the air."

Although Ott had been wearing glasses since 1941, when he discarded his warm-up bat and settled into his left-handed stance at home plate, I was surprised to see that the famous player was bespectacled. For a nine-year-old, anyone 38 and wearing glasses *must be over the hill!* But I instinctively liked him and it was sure "goose bump time" to see the legendary right leg poised in the air, as Mel began his swing—a home run would tie the game! But, alas, the storied right fielder managed only a foul pop corralled easily by the St. Louis third baseman, Whitey Kurowski, to end the inning.

It suddenly dawned on me, while researching this essay, that my dad and I had witnessed the final at-bat of perhaps the most beloved player in the history of the New York Giants!

Early Years of a Young Mel Ott

Melvin Thomas Ott let out an ear-splitting scream when he was smacked in the backside a few minutes past 7 PM on March 2, 1909, in the family home at Gretna, Louisiana, the product of Charles and Caroline Ott. He was a whopping twelve pounds with a pair of lungs to match his weight.

Gretna, just across the Mississippi from New Orleans, was a wonderful place for a growing boy. Shortly after his sixteenth birthday, while catching for his high school team, things started to fall into place rapidly for Master Melvin. He was introduced to Harry P. Williams, a wealthy timber tycoon who owned a semi-pro team operating at his sprawling estate in Paterson, Louisiana. Ott caught for the Paterson Grays who barnstormed around the small towns in the area, for $150 a month and immediately exploded as a star power hitter, crushing mammoth shots all over the circuit.

Enter John McGraw

Williams was a great friend of John Joseph McGraw and sent off a telegram to the volatile Giants manager. He had a boy who would be a sure-fire major league slugger. Soon, on a September New York morning in 1925, the trembling youth was face-to-face with the notorious Little Napoleon. He put down his straw suitcase, stuck out his quivering right hand, and announced, "Mr. McGraw, I'm Mel Ott."

"Muggsy" knew Ott was not big enough to catch for him, but the feisty titan only needed to see the kid rip one line drive after another to right field to know he was a keeper. McGraw turned to his Hall of Fame second baseman, Frankie Frisch, and blurted to the Fordham Flash,

> "Did you see that? He's just like one of those golfers that never takes his eye off the ball. His whole body moves, but his head doesn't. That's the best natural swing I've seen in years!"

For a variety of reasons—it could never happen in today's game—McGraw kept his prize 16-year-old on the bench with him for two years, mentoring him and using him as an occasional right fielder and pinch hitter. Mel later said, "McGraw taught me three lasting lessons: hustle, be aware, and always anticipate the next play."

The manager even brought in a world-class sprinter, Bernie Wefers, to teach his youthful protégé how to run. Ott amplifies, "Wefers killed me with wind sprints. But he showed me how to keep my heavy legs from cramping by running more on my toes." McGraw was also a fanatic on proper sliding into a base. Ott used to wad up pillows in his hotel room, dash across the floor, and take off feet first. During a card game, with loud thumps coming from the room overhead, one veteran Giant grinned and said, "Little Sunshine is stealing bases again!"

After a couple of years playing part-time, benefitting from the master's tutelage on the Giants bench, then returning to high school to pursue his diploma, Mel Ott became the regular right fielder for John McGraw's team in 1928, at the age of 19. Feared in the clutch, he poled 18 homers that year and expertly played caroms off the tricky right-field wall at the Polo Grounds.

Mel's Career Takes Off

Through 1945, through the depression, the New Deal, and World War 11, Ott led the league in homers six times, walks six times (he had exactly 100 walks three consecutive years, '39, '40, '41), on-base percentage four times, OPS + five times, and WAR (wins above replacement) four times. As Gary Livacari observes in his excellent essay (Jan. 2017) some pooh-poohed Ott's homer total, pointing out 63 percent of them were hit at the PG, where it was only 257 feet down the right-field line. Melvin responded, "If it was so easy, why didn't more do it?" It wasn't that easy. A hitter had to pull the ball sharply to park it over the Gem Razor Blade sign near the foul line. In the unique park, right field suddenly became 395 feet.

The genius of Mel Ott was his ability to maximize the full power of his 5'9" 165-pound frame by perfectly leveraging his leg kick and dropping his bat a split second before contacting the ball. This worked at the Polo Grounds, more so later in his career. After 1941, he hit 100 of his 123 home runs at home. But in the early years, it wasn't quite so lopsided. In his breakout 1929 campaign, Mel smashed 22 of his 42 homers away from the friendly 155th St. venue. On the road, Ott altered his approach, batting 14 points higher (.311/.297) with many more doubles and triples. "He bloomed where he was planted," as my wife, Susan, likes to say.

Mel Ott got mixed reviews as a Giants manager. But everyone was crushed by his untimely death, resulting from a car crash on a fog-shrouded Mississippi road in 1958. Worshipped by his wife, Mildred, and two daughters, sportswriter Arnold Hano summed up the thoughts of many,

"When he died he held 14 baseball records. A little man with a bashful smile and a silken swing, he was baseball's legendary nice guy. His death was the worst that could have happened to baseball, but his playing career had been the best."

June 15, 2022

Sources: *Sport Magazine*, June 1948, "Mel Ott On The Hot Seat" by Al Stump; SABR article, "Mel Ott," by Fred Stein; James Montemurro: "Greatest Baseball Fan"; Stat Stories, Forgotten Stars, Bobby; 100 Greatest Baseball Players, Joe Posnanski; Mel Ott baseball reference.com; NY Giants 1947 schedule almanac

BOBO NEWSOM: A GREAT CHARACTER WITH A HEART TO MATCH

He bestrode the baseball firmament like a colossus--both physically at 6'3" 220 pounds, and with a flamboyant, fill-the-room personality. He often spoke in the third person and called everybody by *one name* because he couldn't be bothered remembering his teammates' real names. That name, "Bobo," became his nickname.

Bobo Newsom's pitching career spanned four decades ('29-'53) with nine teams, including all three New York teams. When he was with the Giants, in 1948, he came in from the bullpen to relieve the starting pitcher one afternoon at the Polo Grounds. As he approached the mound, where Giants catcher Walker Cooper was engaged, he said, "Coop, you have a kind face." The big back stop replied with a smile, "Really?" Bobo shot back, "Yeah, the kind I'd like to step on!" But no harm was intended. He thrived on being outrageous and most people took him in stride. In fact, all he really wanted was to be loved by everybody. He was especially kind to rookies, often treating them to dinner and sharing words of wisdom.

Teammate Charlie Gehringer related in an interview, "He was quite a kidder and would drive guys nuts who weren't quick with the repartee. He did an incredible "Amos and Andy" imitation and if you weren't looking at him, you'd swear you were listening to the radio. He drank beer with the best of them, but he was a good pitcher with a great arm and a big heart for the game."

His career was one of stark contrasts. He lost 20 games in a season three times, but won 20 three years in a row (1938, '39 and '40). In '38, with a 20-16 mark, he had a 5.08 ERA. Only one other pitcher ever won 20 or more games with an ERA over 5.00. In 1940, his best year, he excelled with a record of 21-5, allowing just 2.83 runs per nine innings. Newsom was proud that he kept his career ERA under 4.00 with a 3.98 final number. However, he was one of only two pitchers to ever post 200 wins (211-222) and finish with a below .500 winning percentage. His stint with the hapless St. Louis Browns didn't help.

Bobo Newsom was also outspoken and could explode in a sudden, bizarre manner. Pitching for the Dodgers in 1943, he was getting thumped by the Pirates and got into it hot and heavy with manager Leo Durocher, about how to pitch to Vince DiMaggio. The Lip finally had enough and suspended his hurler for the rest of the season. But the next day the entire Brooklyn ball club, led by Arky Vaughn, threatened to walk out if Durocher didn't lift the suspension. The fiery skipper relented.

He was selected to four All-Star games and pitched in two World Series. The 1947 Series, when he pitched in relief for the Yankees against the Dodgers, was forgettable at the age of 39. But he was brilliant and heroic in 1940, going 2-1 with three complete games and a scintillating 1.38 ERA--pitching for the Detroit Tigers against the Cincinnati Reds. The

Reds won in a seven game thriller but the real story was Bobo. He opened with a win and then his beloved father suffered a heart attack and passed away a couple of days later. Louis Norman Newsom stayed with the team and proclaimed, "My next start will be dedicated to my dad." He spun a masterful three hitter before 55,000 fans at Briggs Stadium, as Detroit, with an 8-0 win, went ahead three games to two in the Series.

With only one days rest, he asked for the ball in game seven, opposed by Paul Derringer. The result was a taut 2-1 complete game loss, played in one hour 47 minutes, at Crosley Field. But our hero almost propelled his team to a magnificent underdog triumph. Cincy won 100 games that season compared to 90 for the Tigers.

He left us too soon at the age of 55, in 1962, succumbing to a liver ailment. Bobo appeared in the classic poem by Ogden Nash, published in January, 1949, in Sport Magazine titled, Line-Up for Yesterday an ABC of Baseball Immortals. The only player highlighted who is not in the Hall of Fame. There are those, however, who think he should be.

April 7, 2023

SOURCES: Bobo Newsom, baseball reference; SABR, Bobo Newsom by Ralph Berger; Bobo by John Howay; Baseball Fever, Bobo, notes from Sliding Billy; Wikipedia, 1940 World Series; Sport Magazine, Jan. '49, Ogden Nash.

SAILING THROUGH THE DECADES WITH THE YANKEE CLIPPER-PART ONE

"The phrase 'off with the crack of the bat,' while romantic, is really meaningless, since the outfielder should be in motion long before he hears the sound of the ball meeting the bat." -Joe DiMaggio

"In the dance you can never aspire to be a Fred Astaire, or in baseball, a Joe DiMaggio-because their feet never touch the ground." -Marty Feldman

My dad told me: "DiMaggio never made a great catch. He was always there waiting."

It was Joe DiMaggio's last World Series, Mickey Mantle's and Willie Mays' first. And, as the Yankees took their positions for Game Two, with the great Joe D. in center and the rookie "Commerce Comet" in right, the 1951 Fall Classic was being broadcast nationwide for the first time, with a coaxial cable linking both coasts.

With 66,000 in the stands, Yanks leading 2-0 in the top of the fifth, Willie Mays swatted a drive to deep right center. Mantle described what happened next:

"I was racing to the ball, not looking up...suddenly, there was Joe standing there already in position to catch the ball! I had to put on the brakes in a hurry and somehow got my cleat caught in a Stadium drain cover. I went down and thought my knee had snapped."

Mickey's father, Mutt Mantle, was in the Yankees dugout and saw his son carried off on a stretcher. Mick suffered a severely sprained knee and would miss the rest of the World Series. Was Joe's amazing ball-tracking radar inadvertently responsible for Mantle's first major injury? DiMaggio said, "After that injury, Mickey never had a day without pain." Be that as it may, let's take a superfast cruise through the Yankee Clipper's remarkable career. Don't go too near the rail now, we don't have time to fish you out of the water!

THE BEGINNING

As a prescient dawn ushered in November 25, 1914, in Martinez, California, Joseph Paul DiMaggio, the eighth of nine children of an Italian immigrant fisherman, seemed to have his historic journey already well-choreographed.

SOME CATCH!

In 1933, with help from his older brother Vince, 18-year-old phenom Joe DiMaggio caught on with the San Francisco Seals and proceeded to dominate the Pacific Coast League, including a 61-game hitting streak. Yankee owner, Col. Jacob Ruppert, shelled out 75 grand (and five players) to put him in the lineup for New York on May 3, 1936, at Yankee Stadium: Crosetti ss, Rolfe 3b, DiMaggio lf, Gehrig 1b, Dickey c, Chapman cf, Selkirk rf, Lazzeri 2b, Gomez p. Joe and Lou combined for seven hits, as the Yankees bombed the St. Louis Browns 14-5.

In his first four years, the Bronx Bombers produced four World Series championships (beating the Giants twice, Cubs and Reds). DiMaggio and The Iron Horse were a formidable one-two punch for three years (especially the first two before ALS) highlighted by Joe's .346 BA, 46 HR, 151 runs scored, and Lou's .354 BA, 49 HR, and 158 RBI.

Lou Gehrig said, "DiMaggio is the greatest hitter I know." Babe Ruth chimed in, "This DiMaggio boy sure looks like a natural to become the No. 1 hitter in the game!" Ty Cobb said simply, "DiMaggio is wonderful."

His stance and swing were classic. One sportswriter described it this way,

"Stood stock still…head never moved with his feet wide apart…very short stride…bat held high and steady with his arms well away from his body…as the pitch approached he rotated his hips, sending power through his perfectly level swing."

The fans appreciated Joe's wonderful talent but…smile already, will ya? Joe projected an aura of unmatched class and graceful application but with none of the trimmings. *Daily News* sports columnist, Jimmy Powers, wrote, "DiMaggio made a mistake by rebuffing the friendly gestures of teammates Tony Lazzeri and Frank Crossetti when he first came up. 'Leave him alone, boys,' said Push-'Em-Up one afternoon. 'He knows it all.' " In time, though, players and fans alike began to understand the shy, quiet superstar.

A Movie Star, an MVP and More…

Joltin' Joe was in love - he'd met Dorothy Arnold, a beautiful blond starlet, in the fall of 1937 when she and Joe "starred" in the forgettable film, Manhattan Merry-Go-Round. They were now an *item*.

After Joe's first Most Valuable Player Award in 1939, sparked by a .381 batting title, Joe and Dorothy were married on November 19. (Soon thereafter, however, the young bride began to sense Joe's increasing aloofness). A second BA crown followed in '40, as the Clipper's barrel connected to the tune of .352 with an American League-best OPS+ mark of 173. But the team fell into an inexplicable hitting slump, a bottom rung .259, and finished two games behind Detroit in third place.

A Year for the Books

1941 saw the infamous December 7; Glenn Miller topped the Big Band charts; America flocked to see "The Maltese Falcon;" Ted Williams hit an astonishing .406; and Joe D. was blessed with a beautiful son, Joseph Paul DiMaggio III. Dad also hit in 56 consecutive games.

It started May 15 with a single off lefty Ed Smith of the White Sox. It ended July 17 against Cleveland's Al Smith (another southpaw) and Jim Bagby. First time up DiMag lashed a vicious grounder that third baseman Ken Keltner backhanded brilliantly near the foul line. "Low curve, I hit it pretty good," said Joe. "Keltner actually caught the ball behind him. I never thought he'd get it."

Joe had mixed emotions. "Naturally I wanted to keep it going, but I have to admit it was quite a strain. The main thing is we won the game." (*must read*: Gary Livacari's essays on The Streak and more about the brothers D.)

The Yankees beat the Dodgers four games to one in a World Series that included the famous Mickey Owen missed third strike to Tommy Henrich in Game Four. Joe won his second MVP, besting Teddy Ballgame 291-254 in the voting. The Clipper was at his peak now, gliding to balls in the outfield as if on an ethereal magic carpet, while batting .357 and sporting a league-high 125 RBI.

After a seventh straight 100+ RBI season and a loss to St. Louis in the '42 Series, DiMaggio enlisted in the Army. His wife filed for divorce during his second year in the service. "He acted like a bachelor and chose not to talk to me for days at a time. He spent his entire life with his men friends," sobbed a pale Dorothy DiMaggio.

Back home in 1946, Joe moved on stoically and signed more autographs during spring training that year than he'd ever done in his career. DiMaggio had transferred his love to his adoring fans, as well as his young son.

August 5, 2022

Sources: Daily News Legends Series: Joe DiMaggio 1914-1999; Wikipedia, Dorothy Arnold; Wikipedia, Joe DiMaggio; Baseball Ref, Lou Gehrig; Baseball Ref; Joe DiMaggio; Mickey Mantle's Worst Injury, Harold Friend; Wikipedia, 1951 World Series; Google search: Joe DiMaggio and Ted Williams, contrasting swings.

JOE DIMAGGIO, PART TWO DiMAG POST-WAR: JOE, MARILYN, AND PAUL SIMON

"It was a very tough team. It was a team where everyone demanded complete effort. We led the league in RA's—Red Asses—that's the baseball term for very tough, hard guys. We had more than anyone in the league. Even DiMaggio-elegant as hell, beautiful clothes, always a suit, a gent—but on the field he was a real RA."-Gene Woodling.

Joe's three-year hitch in the army was not arduous, "I spent my entire time in the war in Hawaii. I had developed stomach ulcers and they put me in the special services. We played a lot of ball over there and it wasn't bad duty. The war took a lot more out of guys like Ted Williams and Bob Feller." DiMaggio felt so guilty he asked to be transferred to combat duty in his third year. The request was denied.

He was a more affable star in 1946, signing autographs by the dozens. But DiMag batted only .290 in his first year back. "Obviously I was not the same player I was after I came out of the war," Joe said. "All you have to do is look at the record." In the seven years before his service interruption, the Clipper had a composite .340 batting average, averaged 133 RBI per season, and, for five consecutive years, hit an average of 34 home runs.

1947 was injury-riddled: March bone spur, July pulled leg muscle, August torn neck muscle followed by a heel issue. Homers and RBI were virtually the same but his batting average improved 25 points to .315. Joe Trimble, *New York Daily News* sports columnist, crystalized Joltin' Joe's value, "DiMaggio is an inspiration to the rest of the club. They just seem to pick up and go into high gear when he shows the way."

The Bucky Harris-led Yanks cruised to the pennant over Detroit and then beat Brooklyn in a heart-stopping seven games in the first televised World Series. Game Four was historic: Bill Bevens pitched 8 2/3 innings of no-hit ball and then gave up Cookie Lavagetto's double off the right screen for the win. The classic Red Barber call, in his gentle southern tone, lives on:

"*Heah*" comes the tying run…and "*heah*" comes the winning run! And the Dodgers are killin' Lavagetto!

DiMag won his third MVP in '47 beating Ted Williams by a single vote, 202 to 201. Williams buried DiMaggio in every hitting statistic, leading the American League in no less than ten categories, with a whopping OPS+ mark of 205. That's 105% better than the average player! But just enough writers agreed with Trimble. Joe would spank a pitch off his ear for the game-winning double—Williams would take a ball barely out of his "sweet zone" and walk to first base.

OH, THE SUMMER OF '49!

The Bombers didn't win in 1948, so naturally Bucky Harris was fired. Joe D. had a better year, batting .320 and leading the league with 39 home runs and 155 RBI. Casey Stengel took over the helm in 1949 and the Yankees went on to win a record five straight World championships. Many thought 'Ol Case was a genius. But the Bombers were so loaded my aunt Tillie could have made out the line-up cards, milked her cows, and won going away.

The pennant race between the Yankees and Red Sox that season was a sizzler to the wire. Two Yankee immortals had been laid to rest during the decade (Gehrig '41 and Ruth '48), and now Joe DiMaggio would reach his heroic zenith in a baseball campaign to remember. The Yankee Clipper clobbered the Sox in late June, overcoming a missed half season with a calcified spur in his right heel. In the Yankees' three-game sweep at Fenway, Joe hit four homers and drove in nine runs.

But undaunted, powerful Boston went on to win 60 of their next 80 games, and roared into Yankee Stadium on October 1, "Joe DiMaggio Day," [ed. note: *see* featured photo above from "Joe DiMaggio Day"] needing only one victory out of two remaining games to win the pennant. They couldn't do it. After losing 18 pounds battling viral pneumonia most of September, the Clipper had to lean on brother Dom's shoulder during pregame ceremonies. On his special Saturday, Joe's face was an ashen grey and he felt weak as a kitten. Somehow, though, he managed two key hits in a Yankee comeback victory. They outlasted Boston on Sunday, October 2, to win the pennant. It was the saddest day of Ted Williams' career.

Joe batted .381 against the Red Sox in '49. Overall, in 76 games, he hit .346, belted 14 home runs, and slugged 67 runners across home plate. He had an OBP of .459.

A fine 1950 summer was followed by a dismal, aborted season. On Dec. 19, 1951, Joe DiMaggio addressed the press: "I feel like I have reached the stage where I can no longer produce for my club. I was full of aches and pains and it had been a chore for me to play. When baseball is no longer fun, it's no longer a game, and so, I've played my last game of ball."

JOE AND MARILYN!

We know four things about Joe DiMaggio. He was a great player, an intensely private man, not good marriage material—and his only true love was Marilyn Monroe. They met on a blind date arranged by a mutual friend. "When I saw him that first night," said MM, "My first thought was: he's different."

After a quiet romance for two years, they were married in the chamber of a Municipal Court judge in San Francisco, on January 15, 1954. They spent their wedding night in a $4 dollar motel. When he was asked whether his marriage to Marilyn Monroe was going to be good for him, Joe answered, "It's got to be better than rooming with Joe Page."

Marilyn filed for divorce on October 5, 1954, citing incompatibility. Joe hadn't changed since his marriage to actress Dorothy Arnold. He didn't talk to Marilyn for days on end, preferring late-night poker games to her company. Joe admitted, "I know I am wrong in my approach of coldness and indifference. I regret it. But I cannot help it."

The legendary Lexington Avenue skirt-blowing subway scene, filmed in September, pretty much signaled the end. DiMag exclaimed: "What the hell is this?" as he watched 15 takes in front of 1500 onlookers, completing the filming of *The Seven Year Itch*. Joe was livid as he watched his wife "too much exposed" and stormed off the set. Later at home, more than one DiMaggio *love tap* was apparently delivered to the lovely Monroe physiognomy.

But the spark rekindled after the break-up and they were seemingly ready for a second try when Marilyn's sudden death shocked the world on August 6, 1962. Joe D was devastated. Six red roses would occupy a black metal vase, to be placed at her crypt "twice a week, forever" per Joe's instructions.

WHAT DID SIMON SAY?

DiMaggio's success as a spokesman for the Bowery Bank and Mr. Coffee, in the early '70s, was assured by his status as a living legend. Not only by his marriage to MM but also by a mention in Ernest Hemmingway's "The Old Man and the Sea" and a famous lyric in the movie soundtrack for *The Graduate.*

Word was Joe was going to sue Paul Simon for what he perceived to be a mockery in the line, "Where have you gone, Joe Dimaggio…" from the song, "Mrs. Robinson." Simon explained, "I met Joe for the first time in an Italian restaurant on Central Park South in '68 when the song was popular. Joe firmly asked what the line meant since he hadn't gone anywhere. I explained I wasn't making fun of him, it was a metaphor. That Joe was a symbol representing a certain kind of departed hero in America. He understood and everything was cool."

TIDBITS and FINAL THOUGHTS

In addition to his lifetime .325, 361, and 155 OPS+, Joe was an All-Star all 13 years as a Yankee, while his teams captured ten pennants and nine World Series. Furthermore:

- He became the first player to break $100,000 in earnings, in 1949, (70K plus bonuses).
- Three MVP awards ('39, '41, '47).
- Hall Of Fame, 1955.
- Voted Baseball's Greatest Living Player during baseball's Centennial Year, 1969.
- Stole home five times during his career.
- Possibly even more impressive than his 56-game hitting streak, DiMag holds the record for most seasons with more home runs

than strikeouts (min 20 homers). A feat he accomplished seven times! (Berra-5, Kluzewski-4, Dickey-3, Mize-3, O'Doul-3, Williams-3, Gehrig-2)
- From his hospital bed in 1999, Joe triggered the 14-year emotional reunion between George Steinbrenner and Yogi Berra.

His name seems synonymous with class, grace, distance, icon, majesty, mystique, greatness, and team player. He is there forever in Monument Park at Yankee Stadium with Ruth, Gehrig, Huggins, and Mantle.

"I'm just a ballplayer with one ambition—to give all I've got to help my ball club win. I've never played any other way."

August 19, 2022

Sources: Daily News Legends Series, Joe DiMaggio, 1914-1999; Summer Of '49, David Halberstam; Red Sox Schedule Almanac, 1949; Joe D baseball ref; Ted Williams baseball ref; Joe DiMaggio, obit, 1999, NY Times: Yankees schedule almanac, 1949. Google search: DiMaggio spokesman Bowery Bank, Mr. Coffee.

THE CLOWN PRINCE OF BASEBALL: Al SCHACHT

"I came into this world very homely and haven't changed a bit since!" - Al Schacht

"I have become a household word. Whenever I enter a town, a courier gallops madly through the streets and shouts, 'Hey girls - Al Schacht's in town!'"

The name Al Schacht flashes a vivid memory of me and my dad watching The Clown Prince of Baseball at Yankee stadium in 1948. He came out and cavorted around home plate wearing a battered top hat and ridiculous frock coat and carrying a tremendous 25-pound catcher's mitt.

He interacted with a couple of umpires and was very funny. He had just the right moves and craziness to make it work. We'd catch up with The Clown Prince later that day…

Alexander Schacht was born November 11, 1892, in the Bronx on Catharine St., the site that would eventually become Yankee Stadium. Both parents were born in Russia. His father, Samuel Schacht, was a skilled locksmith and an ironworker, once making a set of iron doors for the White House during the Teddy Roosevelt administration. Al's mother, Ida, came from an aristocratic family where her father was the town rabbi.

Early on, young Al burned with a passion to pitch in the major leagues. This was fine with his easygoing father, not so much with his mom. She wanted him to be more like his older brother Louis, who was a fine student. Schacht had a hard time at Commerce High in 1908, consumed with baseball, and harassed by Irish and Italian kids to and from school. He was about 5'9" but weighed only 125 pounds. Pitching was his thing but the coach thought Al was too small and put him at second base. Disaster at the position was putting it mildly. By his own admission, he couldn't hit, field, or run. Eventually, he did pitch effectively for Commerce but school just didn't agree with him and he finally dropped out.

Given an unexpected green light from both parents, Al accepted an offer to play semi-pro baseball for the Walton, NY Rifraffs for four dollars a week and board. It was at Walton that Schacht first took up clowning. He would hilariously impersonate a pitcher who was getting belted all over the park, but who refused to go to the shower when the manager came to take him out. The fans loved it and Al continued performing his pantomime at every town social event.

From Walton, Schacht hooked up with the Cleveland team in the outlaw United States league. In a relief stint, he struck out 11 of 15 batters and went on to win five straight games. But, alas, the team folded at the end of the season. Now what? Out of baseball, Al would go to a local gym to work out and do some boxing. Then fate intervened when a cousin from Boston called and wanted Al to manage a talented young boxer he knew, named Joe White. The kid could punch but, unbeknownst to Schacht, his connections were not exactly lily-white. As he walked toward the ring for a big fight with his new boxer, Al suddenly felt a hard object pressed against his back. A voice said, "Take one more step and you're a dead pigeon." Ring management over, baby!

After his father died of pneumonia in 1913, Al fought intense grief and managed to make the Newark Indians in the International League. He was on the staff of a pennant-winning team that year. Two good years followed with Al winning 25 games. But then a sore arm plagued him for two years, finally incapacitating him, as WW 1 raged abroad and involved the United States in 1917. Schacht was inducted in 1918, despite a hearing deficiency. But he remained in the States playing baseball.

Returning to the International League in '19, with the Jersey City Little Giants, Schacht, now with a sound arm, led the IL with nine shutouts, posted a 1.95 ERA, and won 19 games for a team that went 37-76. Bombarding Washington Senator's owner, Clark Griffith, with letters touting his pitching accomplishments, Schacht so intrigued the baseball magnate that Griffith personally scouted him. In late 1919, Al Schacht realized his dream of pitching in the big leagues! Not helped by a freak broken shoulder in 1920, from 1919-1921 his slate showed a record of 14-10, 197 innings, eight complete games, one shutout, 4.48 ERA. Al bragged that Babe Ruth never homered off him. Injuries ended his major league career but still hungry to pitch, at only 29, Schacht hung on for three more decent seasons with Reading, Binghamton, and New Haven.

He re-joined the Senators as a third base coach in 1925 and stayed on for a decade. While with Washington, Schacht met former major league star Nick Altrock, who was the then reigning number one clown in baseball. Although the two personalities clashed harshly, they formed a great two-man comedy act. With help from John McGraw, they opened with a bang during the 1922 World Series between the Yankees and the Giants.

In 1934, late in the season, player-manager Joe Cronin broke his wrist shortly after getting married. Griffith gave him the rest of the year off and Al Schacht became the Senators interim manager for one month. Both were traded to the Boston Red Sox at season's end, and that ended the partnership between Altrock and Schacht. Al Schacht was now on his own and the official Clown Prince of Baseball.

Schacht thrived after his coaching career ended. Overall, he entertained at 25 World Series, 18 All-star games and performed for the USO in World War II in Europe, Asia, and Africa - many times under enemy fire. Among his delightful hilarities were mock weddings at home plate, shadowing the third baseman, and reading newspapers while sitting on the base paths. He also wrote four books, including *Clowning through Baseball*.

...After the game, my dad took me to Al Schacht's restaurant on E. 52nd Street. We enjoyed a delicious meal and then The Clown Prince arrived. I had spotted a miniature bat autographed by Al. My father approached Mr. Schacht, "Al, I brought my little boy all the way from Westfield NJ to see you today at the Yankee game and we just had a great dinner. Do you think you could give him that bat as a souvenir?" Al was not happy about parting with the little beauty free of charge. This surprised me, being such an adorable child. [*Ed. note: Haha!*] But a little more prodding prompted the funny man to hand it over-reluctantly. I loved that bat!

Here's some amusing stuff on Al Shacht's "Score Card' menu: Pepper Martin Steak, Dizzy Trout, Connie Mackerel. Or how about Duck Medwick, Vitt Appling Sauce, or Chicken a la Clyde King? For dessert, enjoy Pie Traynor, Yogi Berries, Napolean Lajoie, or Del Rice pudding. On the back of the menu—"Try our Oysters. If you find a pearl, you might break even."

Alexander Schacht passed in 1984 at 91, survived by his wife, Maybelle.

"He was born with a gift of laughter and a sense that the world was mad."

January 12, 2022

Sources: Beer Drinkers and Hell Raisers-Al Schacht; Bullpen Front Page-Al Schacht; Rafael Sabatini-Scaramouche; Al Schacht-Baseball Reference.com; Al Schact/SABR/article/Ralph Berger; Al Schacht, Wikipedia pages; Al Schact's "Score Card" Restaurant Menu

THE SHOT HEARD 'ROUND THE WORLD (THAT ALMOST WASN'T)

Let's go directly to Shibe Park in Philadelphia, September 30, where the Dodgers faced the Phillies in the last regular season game of the '51 season. The day's action began with both the Giants and Dodgers posting records of 95-58.

Preacher Roe started for Brooklyn, a scintillating 22-3 on the year, and was opposed by Bubba Church, a 15-game winner for the Phillies. Both the crafty left-hander and right-handed curveball artist were having their best seasons. But this was not to be either pitcher's finest hour.

Roe was sent to the showers in the second inning, as Philadelphia jumped out to a 4-0 lead. The pennant-winning Whiz Kids of 1950 added two more and led 6-1 in the fourth. Brooklyn bounced Bubba the next inning and closed the gap to 6-5. But the "Fightin' Phils," sparked by a Bill "Swish" Nicholson triple, tallied two more and padded the lead to 8-5 at the end of five innings.

Now, the Brooklyns were watching the scoreboard intently. And, as the teams took the field for the sixth inning, the stark reality of the situation hit them right between the eyes: the Giants had beaten the Braves 3-2 behind Larry Jansen. My dad liked Longfellow's observation, "Life is real! Life is earnest!" I doubt the Dodgers were thinking of Henry Wadsworth at the time but they knew if they didn't get after it in a hurry the season would be over. The Jints were leading the National League now by a half-game!

Giants fans desperately did not want any part of those bruising guys who played ball southeast of the historic Gowanus Canal. I was one of those fans, never hating Dem Bums, but scared to death of that wrecking crew in a showdown series. If only the Phillies could hold on!

With one gone in the Dodgers' eighth, Hodges and Cox singled and both came home on a Rube Walker double. Now it was 8-7 and manager Eddie Sawyer brought in his 21-game winner, Robin Roberts, to pitch to Carl Furillo. The Phil's ace had pitched eight innings the day before in a 5-0 loss to Brooklyn and would log 315 innings that year. But it was no holds barred now. Furillo promptly cracked a single to left to plate pinch runner, Don Thompson, knotting the game at eight. Roberts settled in and retired the side.

Manager Charlie Dressen countered with his workhorse star, Don Newcombe, who had spun a seven-hit shutout only 24 hours earlier. The two 20-game winners held their opponents in check into extra innings, with Roberts retiring 10 consecutive Dodgers at one point. The tension mounted by the minute in the bottom of the 12th as Roberts, hitting for himself, led off with a walk. Eddie Pellagrini laid down a perfect sac bunt and Roberts was safe at second, with Pellagrini aboard at first. On a hit-and-run, always clutch Richie Ashburn lashed a bullet two-hopper to Gil Hodges, who made the unassisted putout at first base. With one out, both runners advanced to third and second, respectively. Willie "Puddin' Head" Jones was walked intentionally to load the bases. Del Ennis struck out. The stage was set for the Dodger play of the season.

Jackie Saves the Day!

First baseman, Eddie Waitkus looped a humpback liner to the right of second, headed for center field—to apparently end the ballgame. But Robinson, although notoriously slow going to his right, dove headlong through the air reaching across his body with his glove hand, inches above the ground, landing hard on his right shoulder with the ball incredibly nestled in his glove! He rolled over and curiously tossed the baseball toward second base, as if attempting to get a force play. (He lay motionless for minutes near the outfield grass before moving). Robin Roberts, running from third with the potential winning run, was certain Jackie had trapped the ball. But umpire, Lon Warneke, raised his right hand and called Waitkus out to end the inning. The Phillies bench erupted and screamed as one that the ball had been trapped and not caught cleanly.

Roberts was breezing as the game entered the 14th inning. Reese and Snider both popped out. Jackie Robinson, still in the game miraculously, stepped into the batter's box and took a ball and a strike. Roberts then unleashed a high fastball on the inside part of the plate. Robinson smashed it into the upper deck in left field and Roberts had yielded his 20th home run of the season. Brooklyn 9, Philadelphia 8. Roy Campanella doubled but stayed at second.

"What did the umpire say?..."

In their last licks, Ashburn clipped Bud Podbielon for a single. However, the game ended as Waitkus lofted a soft fly to Andy Pafko in left field. But did Jackie Robinson really catch that Eddie Waitkus liner in the twelfth inning? The Phillies, to a man, claimed he did not. Roberts believed that Jack's wild toss from a prone position toward second base showed that Robinson thought he had trapped the ball and was futilely trying for the force play at second. During the off-season, Robin spotted Jackie at a winter banquet. He said, "Jackie you didn't catch the ball Waitkus hit." Robinson grinned and asked, "What did the umpire say?"

Had there been instant replay back in the day, things might have been different. Instead of Bobby Thomson being the hero of a historic playoff series with two game-winning home runs—including, The Shot Heard 'Round the World—he might be remembered as a good player who was part of a memorable pennant race and the only major leaguer to be born in Scotland.

February 4, 2023

Sources: "Robinson saved the Dodgers," author, C. Paul Rogers 111; Box Score, Phila., Brooklyn, 9/30/51; Sched almanac, 1951, Giants/Dodgers; Roberts, Church, Roe, baseball ref.com; Wikipedia: Brooklyn.

AN UMPIRE'S UMPIRE

From the vast photo archives of Baseball History Comes Alive, we've projected a stunning, 10 by 18 foot picture on our auditorium screen. A collective gasp emanates from a small group of fans, as they take in the image. It's not the diminutive 5'7" 165 pound physical presence but the overwhelmingly confident, feisty, take charge smile, projecting total control. Mess with this guy at your own risk. He fears nothing.

Ironically, "Jocko" Conlan got his nickname from another major league player with the same name, but with a single letter changed in the surname. Jocko Con*lin* played briefly for the 1923 Boston Braves, as a middle infielder. He was two years older. Both were the same height. Both lived to be 89. There was also a striking facial resemblance. Conlan was at first baffled by the same first name nickname that attached to him but later admitted, "It was the damnedest thing, but I guess I really did look like him. I'd be stopped on the street and somebody would shout, 'Hey, Jocko, remember me from graduate school?' Or, 'Don't you remember me from Harvard?' When I'd look at them in disbelief, they thought I was putting them on!"

The Beginning

Born in 1899, and one of nine children whose dad was a Chicago policeman, Jocko grew up as a rabid Chicago White Sox fan with a burning ambition to play for the pale hose. He would realize that dream, briefly, in 1934. His professional baseball career began in 1920 and included nine years at the highest minor league level (designated AA at the time). He played for the Rochester Tribe, Newark Bears, Toledo Mud Hens and Montreal Royals—batting over .300 six times and never lower than .283. Conlan was fast, with a strong left arm and could go get 'em with the best. He averaged 20 assists a year for several seasons. False modesty was not part of his arsenal. While playing for Rochester, he once tracked a ball from centerfield, up a terrace in left center, scaled wooden boards fronting the fence, whirled and made a lunging one-handed stab--then slid down the wall on his back completing the play. John stated, matter-of-factly, "I don't believe there has ever been a catch quite like that one."

Jocko loved George Stallings who ran the Tribe at the time. Stallings really knew the game. He was tough but fair and presented a handsome, well dressed image, managing in a business suit instead of a uniform. George appreciated his left handed centerfielder, even though he lacked power, because Conlan reminded him of his Miracle 1914 Boston Braves players, who came from last place on July fourth to sweep the mighty Philadelphia Athletics in the World Series. Stallings never let his players talk to an opposition player. He declared, "You're here to beat them, not talk to them. If you want to discuss fishing or hunting, talk about it during the off season. Not here. Not during the season."

In 1925, Stallings had it set up to give Jocko his major league break. Cincinnati would ship three players and $17,500 to Rochester for him. But the day before he was to report his left knee freakishly caught the opposing catcher's shin guard while scoring a run and tore up a gazillion ligaments. It took nine more years for him to make the big leagues. In those days, the majors wouldn't touch a player with a bad knee (except Joe DiMaggio). Jocko's knee was perfect the very next year, but no dice. Oh, the vicissitudes of life.

A New Career Blossoms

Jocko Conlan was now 35 and in his twilight years as a player. Over two limited campaigns with the Chisox, managed by Jimmy Dykes, he batted .263, produced 96 hits and drove home 31 runners. Then in 1935, fate moved its huge hand. During a game with the St. Louis Browns, umpire Red Ormsby suffered heat stroke. In those days, only two umpires covered regular season games. Since no other umpire was available, and John had impeccable integrity, he was asked to work the bases. He had a natural feel for the job—positioning and calling plays quickly with authority. Also, he could run faster than most of the players. Rave notices poured in. And, after a few years of minor league seasoning (at $300/month), a wonderful umpiring career spanned a quarter century in the National League, from 1941 through 1965.

The pint sized arbiter had strong convictions, commanded enormous respect and was unwavering on certain things, particularly checked swings. "To me it was usually crystal clear when a batter swung or didn't swing. An umpire shouldn't have to ask for help on the call." In the early 50's, the field mikes were so close to the action you could sometimes hear stuff you shouldn't hear. Alvin Dark was batting one afternoon at the Polo Grounds when Conlan was behind the plate. He called Alvin out on a checked swing. Clear as a bell, as I watched on TV, Dark screamed in his high pitched Oklahoma twang, "God----it, Jocko, ah heeld up!"

"And I never fell for a catcher moving his mitt to bring a pitch into the strike zone, Conlan emphasized, "A pitch had to be a strike. None of that fancy mitt manipulation ever influenced me!"

The Nice and Not So Nice

According to Jocko, umpires loved Rogers Hornsby. Even though The Rajah had a generally surly disposition, he never argued a call. Yogi Berra was known as a constant grumbler. Stan Musial and Gil Hodges were the best (*so true, having interviewed Gil myself at Shea, in 1968*). Ted Williams, despite his bad press, was held in high esteem by the umps. Jock shared this, "I called Ted out on strikes in the 1947 All-Star game, batting against Ewell Blackwell. The pitch was too low and I knew I blew it. Williams said nothing: he just put his bat on his shoulder and walked back to the dugout. He never brought up the horrendous call and we had a great relationship."

"Jackie Robinson was a fierce competitor, tremendous clutch hitter, the best base runner I ever saw. But he used horrible language. I never tolerated abusive name calling directed at me, that's a sure way to lose respect. One time Jackie thought I missed a play at first. He bellowed from his position at second base, 'Conlan, you so-and-so, you're never in position to make a call!' I said, 'Well, I'm in the perfect position…get out!' He could rile me alright."

"Leo Durocher was worse. At his best, Leo was the game's best manager. But you can have him. His mouth was just awful and he complained about every call against his team. I've had some experience fighting…and I was ready to knock him out once in a game…fortunately, he retreated to the dugout. Not a moment too soon, I might add!"

Conlan praised the skills of black players he saw who never got to the big leagues. "They had marvelous players, those colored teams" he said. "No question, many would have been stars in the majors."

SOME CATCH!

John Bertrand umpired in five World Series and six All-Star games and was inducted into the HOF in the summer of '74, preceded only by Bill Klem and Tommy Connolly, in the arbiter category.

Nattily attired with his blue cap and dandy bow tie, and sporting an outside chest protector, he created an indelible image for those who saw him. Plus, he was the only ump to signal with his left hand--would that he could be signaled back into the game today.

April 28, 2023

Sources: Book: "Jocko," Jocko Conlan & Robert W. Creamer; Wikipedia, Jocko Conlan; Jocko Conlon, baseball ref; Jocko Conlan baseball ref; Alvin Dark, baseball reference

EDDIE STANKY: *THE BRAT!*

"He can't hit, he can't field and he can't run, but I wouldn't trade him for any second baseman in the league."- Leo Durocher, speaking of "The Brat," Eddie Stanky

Edward Raymond Stankiewicz came into the world on September 3, 1915 courtesy of Frank and Anna, who shortened the family name to Stanky when Eddie was a boy. In the tough, blue-collar Philadelphia neighborhood of Kensington, Eddie developed the win-at-all-costs attitude that propelled him to a major league baseball career, despite limited natural talent.

In his senior year at Philadelphia's northeast high school Eddie batted only .243. But his coach, Lester Owen, expressed the essential core of the small firebrand, "He said he was going to be a pro baseball player and that was that. No one doubted him. He was an ordinary boy with extraordinary ambition."

Stanky was signed by the Philadelphia Athletics, and feeling like he must have been trapped inside a pinball machine, Stanky had played shortstop, second, third-and even pitched in his first two years in the class C minor leagues.

After another brief stop, early in the 1939 season Stanky was sent to the Macon Peaches of the class B South Atlantic League, where 14-year major leaguer Milt

Stock was the manager and part owner of the team. Stock told Stanky to curb his temper and stop getting thrown out of games 20 times a year. He installed him as his leadoff hitter and told his diminutive trouble maker to "Get on base anyway you can." It worked. Eddie had three fine years with Macon and made the All-Star team in 1940.

The 5' 7" 150 pounder also found a bride. Milt's daughter, Myrtle "Dickie" Stock, was mesmerized by the pint sized infielder and they were married on April 11, 1942. Dickie was a real Georgia peach, a brunette beauty. In fact, she'd been offered a movie contract by Metro Goldwin Mayer!

Shortly after the wedding, Stock dealt his new son-in-law to the Milwaukee Brewers of the American association, where Stanky enjoyed his best and last minor league season. He copped the batting crown (.342) and was named the league's MVP. Eddie's manager at Milwaukee was Charlie Grimm. In 1943, the Cubs made Grimm their manager and Stanky followed his skipper to Chicago.

At this point, I'll add two personal notes about our irrepressible Brat. In 1950, my dad and I were in the upper deck behind home plate watching the Giants play the Dodgers at the Polo Grounds, on a steamy July afternoon. Stanky hit a bullet to right field for a clean single (or so it appeared). In a series of split second impressions, we then saw Eddie sprint out of the batter's box…wondered why he was running for his life on a routine single…watched Brooklyn right fielder Carl Furillo scoop the ball on one hop and fire a seed to Gil Hodges at first. Stanky was out by an eyelash, but Hodges couldn't hold the powerful throw uncorked by The Reading Rifle at such close range. Stanky was safe!

The play made a lasting impression. Stanky was always in the game, always thinking, always hustling. That's why fans loved him whatever uniform he wore.

In the third game of the 1951 Giants vs. Yankees World Series at the Polo Grounds, fifth inning, Eddie was a dead duck on a pitch out, sliding into second base. But he kicked the ball out of Phil Rizzuto's glove to spark the Giants' winning rally. Rizzuto thought it was interference and also swore Stanky never touched second base and should have been called out. Phil always hated Eddie for embarrassing him.

In the early 90's, I worked with Rizzuto on several Money Store TV commercials. I was all set to ask him about the play but heard him suddenly roar from a distance, "Oh, that Stanky!" That was it. I was afraid to risk ruining our good relationship!

On April 21, 1943, in the first inning of his major league debut Stanky was promptly beaned by Pittsburgh's Rip Sewell. He of the famous Blooper Ball, Sewell didn't throw very hard so it wasn't serious. Years earlier, however, in the minors, he was hit in the head by a pitch that caused a severe concussion resulting in hearing loss, which kept him out of the armed services.

Eddie had a mediocre season with the Cubs in '43 and manager Charlie Grimm traded him to the Dodgers in mid-1944. Eddie set a then major league record in 1945 with 148 walks, as well as denting the dish with 128 runs scored. Loving Dodger fans gave him various nicknames: Stinky, Muggsy, The Walkin' Man and The Brat. The latter stuck, due to Stanky's combative nature and all-out competitiveness.

In 1946, he again led the league in walks with 137 and a marvelous .437 OBP. The following season saw the cantankerous second sacker enjoy his best year in the field, committing only 12 errors, and leading the Dodgers into the World Series. And despite writings to the contrary, Eddie was a champion of Jackie Robinson in 1947. His son, Mike, revealed:

"Dad always talked about that first game and Robinson's enormous talent. He and Jackie became very close, realizing though different in many ways, they shared an intense winning spirit."

However, the brilliant but miserly Branch Rickey was at it again. Almost on the heels of peddling "The People's Cherce" Dixie Walker to Pittsburgh, The Mahatma of Montague Street, again needed the feel of a buck in his pocket and sold Eddie Stanky to the Boston Braves in early 1948 for 40k and two bench players. Dodger fans rattled their cages and carried placards of disapproval as two of their all-time favorites were ripped away in almost rapid fire succession.

Stanky thrived for two years in Beantown, with an all-star first half in '48, until he broke his ankle. The Brat commented that his beloved former manager Leo Durocher, "will be the first horizontal manager in the history of baseball if he bothers me. I'll hit so many foul balls at him… he'll manage lying on the dugout floor." Eddie made hitting foul balls an art form. Braves' coach Johnny Cooney testified:

"We always hated to see him come up in the late innings of a tough game. He'd *think his way to first base*, and the next thing you knew, the panic was on. One day we were riding him pretty hard from the bench. He spotted the loudest of the hecklers and almost tore his head off with a foul drive!"

In 1949, Boston manager, Billy Southworth, morphed into a precursor to Captain Queeg in the dugout. He drove his team relentlessly, trying to win a second consecutive pennant. Some players thought Stanky was trying to take over the club and dissention rippled through the ranks. This resulted in one of the great trades at season's end: Stanky and Alvin Dark to the Giants for Sid Gordon, Willard Marshall, Buddy Kerr and scrub pitcher Sam "Red" Webb. Dark and Stanky revitalized the Giants and only Gordon produced for the Braves.

Reunited with Leo Durocher, Muggsy had his best year in 1950: 144 walks and a whopping .460 OBP to lead the majors, along with an even .300 batting average. No need to review the following season. Suffice it to say kindred souls Eddie and Leo reveled in their finest baseball moment, doing a wrestle/dance down the Polo Grounds' third base line on October 3, 1951.

Stanky got his long awaited opportunity to manage in 1952. The St. Louis Cardinals sent fading pitcher Max Lanier and light hitting speedster Chuck Diering to the Giants. Eddie won the Sporting News Manager of the Year. He also got high marks for piloting the Chicago White Sox in 1967, in a wild four team pennant race.

However, back home in Alabama in 1969, Stanky was to embark on his greatest success. As a baseball coach at the University of Southern Alabama, over the next 14 years, his teams went 488-193. Eddie softened his hard-nosed philosophy on the field to an "everyone plays" style, and transformed the little school into a Sun Belt Conference baseball power, sending 43 players to the major leagues:

"My most wonderful feeling of satisfaction was when mothers would tearfully embrace me at graduation for helping their sons. You can't weigh that."

Eddie Stanky succumbed to a heart attack, June 6, 1999. Many fans remember him fondly as one of the biggest little men in baseball.

September 10, 2021

Sources: *Sport Magazine;* August, 1948, *"How does Stanky do It?"* by Dave Egan; Eddie Stanky Baseball Reference

ONE MEMORABLE OPENING DAY AND STORY

"There is no sport event like Opening Day baseball, the sense of beating back the forces of darkness and the National Football League."- George Vecsey

"There's nothing like Opening Day. There is nothing like the start of a new season. I started playing baseball at seven, quit at 40. It's in my blood." –George Brett

"I'd walk through hell in a gasoline suit to play baseball."-Pete Rose

Baseball Is In the Air!

Well, we're almost there with bubbling over anticipation, when all big-league teams will be in action on one Opening Day, March 30, for the first time since 1968. Fans are already buzzing about the new pitch clock, unveiled in spring training, feeling it will add a needed element of continuity and speed to the game. The odds makers have made the Houston Astros the favorite to win the World Series, with the Mets, Yankees, and Dodgers all close behind. There is a surge of money pouring in on the New York Metropolitans.

A strange phenomenon will soon take place. The first 10 games played will seem to happen slowly. Then the season will get caught in the vortex of its own unique rhythm, and suddenly the All-Star game will be looming right around the corner. Late August will be upon us too soon…footballs in the air…and can our baseball team survive its injuries and make the postseason?

One Vivid Opening Day Memory

April 18, 1952, Opening Day, Ebbets Field. My dad and I, intense Giants fans, along with my best friend, Donn Williams (one of the great Dodgers rooters) were seated in the left field upper deck. It was the first meeting of the two teams since the famous playoff series the year before. Clem Labine, who had shut out the Giants 10-0 at the Polo Grounds, was on the mound. Labine didn't retire a single batter. The Giants KO'd Clem with five runs in the first inning. But Jim Hearn didn't fare much better, lasting only one out in the bottom of the second stanza. The score after two was New York five, Brooklyn four. The teams battled into the twelfth inning tied at six when Andy Pafko homered over the right-center screen off George Spencer to win it for the Brooks, 7-6. From our vantage point, high up in the second deck in left, it looked to me, at first, like a pop fly. But the rising, burgeoning roar from Dodgers fans told a different story.

Fast forward to a TV commercial setting, Thirty years later, at a Staten Island car dealership where I was the spokesman and Willie Mays was one of the sports celebrity guests. A two-minute commercial message would result. In chatting with Willie during a break, I referred to that Opening Day game and said I thought his catch of a Bobby Morgan line drive in the ninth inning was his greatest grab ever. He agreed but then said, "You don't look old enough to remember that. Describe that catch." I launched into the play-by-play:

> "Morgan belted a hard liner into the left-center gap that looked for sure like the game-winner. You came out of nowhere and dove through the air, parallel to the ground, spearing the ball with a supernatural backhand stab. You then hit the ground and rolled over and over again, winding up stretched out on your stomach near the fence and didn't move for several minutes. Both teams rushed to the spot. Jackie Robinson led the Dodgers. Jack confessed, 'We didn't run out there to see if Mays was alright. We couldn't believe he caught the ball!' "

I passed the description test.

It's 2023-But There's Nothing like An Old-Time Baseball Story!

Chester "Red" Hoff was a left-handed pitcher with the Yankees and St. Louis Browns. At the time of the interview in 1991, he was the oldest living major leaguer at 100 years old.

"How I got started? My brother and I were sitting at the dinner table one night. He says 'let's go out and have a little catch.' And I says, 'Oh sure.' "

> "So we went out in the lane and had a little catch and we come back. We didn't say nothing about it. Two days after that he says, 'Let's go out and have another catch.' I says, 'Sure.' And we went out in the lane and had another catch. So we didn't say no more about it. But my brother had something in mind."

> "He says, 'Saturday, we got a game down in Tarrytown, so would you like to go down?' I says, 'Yeah.' I go down and pitch, you know, just for the fun of it. It was in semipro ball and I won the game down there. So it went along alright."

(Hoff had a tryout with the then New York Highlanders and pitched his first big-league game against the Detroit Tigers in 1911).

> "So I got two strikes on the batter. He fouled them off and the catcher gave me a third pitch-out sign. He thought he'd go after a bad ball for the third strike. He didn't go with that. So the catcher come out and he says, 'I'll give you the curve ball sign this time.' "

> "And I gave the batter the best curveball he ever seen and he just looked at it. And the umpire says, 'Strike three and you're out!' And I didn't know who the batter was. So the next morning I picked up a New York Journal and in the sporting page it had in big red letters, HOFF STRIKES OUT COBB. And that started me out in baseball, believe me!"

Over the next four years, Hoff pitched for the Highlanders-Yankees and St. Louis Browns. He pitched 83 innings in the majors, with a 2-2 record and an ERA of 2.49. He lived to be 107.

There is something so comforting about going back into baseball history, enjoying its stories and rich tradition. Writer, Poet Laureate and Red Sox fan, Donald Hall, expressed it perfectly,

> "For most baseball fans, maybe oldest is always the best. We love baseball because it seizes and retains the past, like the snowy village inside a glass paperweight."

But now a new season awaits - and we're ready!

March 5, 2023

Sources: Baseball, an illustrated history, Geoffrey C. Ward and Ken Burns; Wikipedia, Donald Hall; Baseball ref.com, Red Hoff; 1952 Dodgers schedule almanac; Google baseball quotes.

ABOUT THE AUTHOR

Bill Schaefer lives in Springfield, NJ with his wife, Susan. He attended many games with his dad and hung on every pitch with the NY Giants, starting in 1946. Bill graduated from Lehigh University and enjoyed a varied broadcast career, including professional play-by-play, on-camera spokesman, voice over announcer and talk show host. His many radio and magazine interviews include: Willie Mays, Mel Allen, Don Mattingly, Tom Seaver and Bobby Thomson--not to mention, Sen. Strom Thurmond, Jack Benny, Selma Diamond, Liberace and Johnny Cash.